SQUIRES KITCHEN'S GUIDE TO MAKING

sugar
figures

Jan Clement-May

24 fun cake-top characters for every celebration

Dedication

I'd like to dedicate this book in memory of my dear old Nan Ellen, always known affectionately as Nellie. She passed away shortly after reaching the grand old age of 100 whilst I was in the middle of writing this book. She will be sadly missed as she left a rather large hole in my heart but I have many fond memories to cherish.

First published in March 2012 by B. Dutton Publishing Limited, The Grange, Hones Business Park, Farnham, Surrey, GU9 8BB.
Copyright: Jan Clement-May 2012
ISBN-13: 978-1-905113-30-9
All rights reserved.

Publisher: Beverley Dutton
Editor: Jenny Stewart
Art Director/Designer: Sarah Ryan
Deputy Editor: Jenny Royle
Designer: Zena Manicom
Graphic Designer: Louise Pepé
Editorial Assistant: Amy Norman
Photography: Alister Thorpe
Printed in China

With thanks to Sarah Braganza for her contribution to the publishing team

Brownie trefoil and masthead reproduced with kind permission from Girlguiding UK.

Acknowledgements

Special thanks to Rob and Bev for indulging me in my passion of modelling and allowing me to have yet another book under my belt.

To Jenny and Sarah for putting their professionalism and enthusiasm into the book's production, and Alister for the great photography. Brilliant teamwork and a pleasure to work with once again.

introduction

Having completed a book on animal modelling it seemed only natural to follow up with a book on making sugar figures. Tapping into my training from many years ago in model animation has allowed me to create different characters from a selection of professions, hobbies and special celebrations. Each one starts out with basic forms of the human body, adding different shapes and colours for the beginner and working to the more intricate of characters for advanced modellers.

Using the basic shapes of each character over time, having plenty of patience and allowing the different stages to dry as you make the characters will help to build up your confidence with figure modelling. Before long you will develop your own style and design in your own character models to adorn your celebration cakes or cupcakes.

Modelling figures is fun and there doesn't need to be any stress involved, just practice, practice, and more practice! If it looks wrong, try again and for the best results always allow enough time to make the figures as it's not something you can leave to the last minute.

I've had a lot of pleasure in putting the figures together and creating their individual characters. I hope you enjoy making them too – have fun!

Jan
x

contents

recipes

Once you've made your sugar figures you can display them on a celebration cake, on cupcakes or even on cookies. I've suggested a cupcake idea for each of the themes in the book, or you can create your own treats to suit the occasion.

Sponge Cake

Ingredients	15cm (6") round	20.5cm (8") round	12 cupcakes/28 mini
Soft margarine	175g (6oz)	225g (8oz)	115g (4oz)
Caster sugar	175g (6oz)	225g (8oz)	115g (4oz)
Baking powder	8ml (1½tsp)	10ml (2tsp)	5ml (1tsp)
Self-raising flour	225g (8oz)	275g (10oz)	115g (4oz)
Eggs	3	5	2
Milk	25ml (1½tbsp)	30ml (2tbsp)	N/A
Vanilla essence	8ml (1½tsp)	10ml (2tsp)	5ml (1tsp)
Baking time	30 minutes	40 minutes	18–20/12–15 minutes

Variations

Chocolate sponge: add 45ml (3tbsp) of good quality cocoa powder to 60ml (4tbsp) of hot, boiled water and mix. Allow to cool before adding to the cake mixture.

Lemon sponge: add the rind of 2 lemons and 60ml (4tbsp) of lemon juice to the cake mixture.

Orange sponge: add the rind of 2 oranges and 60ml (4tbsp) of orange juice to the cake mixture.

Coffee sponge: add 30ml (2tbsp) of coffee essence to the cake mixture.

Sponge cake method

1 Preheat the oven to 180°C/350°F/gas mark 4. Grease the cake tin(s) and line the base with greaseproof paper or baking parchment. Cut a length of greaseproof paper or baking parchment to fit all the way around the inside of the tin(s).

2 Place all the ingredients into a mixing bowl and beat together in a mixer for approximately 2 minutes (or mix by hand) until well blended. Pour the mixture into the prepared tin(s) and level the top.

3 Bake in the preheated oven for the specified time, or until the cake is firm to the touch and has shrunk away from the sides of the tin. Leave to cool in the tin(s) before turning out onto a cooling rack. Allow to cool completely before decorating.

Cupcake method

1 Preheat the oven to 200°C/400°F/gas mark 6. Place the cupcake cases into a 12-hole bun tin.

2 Place all the ingredients into a mixing bowl and beat together in a mixer for 2 minutes (or mix by hand) until well blended. Half-fill the cake cases with the cake mixture and level the tops.

3 Bake in the preheated oven for around 18–20 minutes, or until the cakes have risen and are firm to the touch. Remove the cakes from the bun tin and leave to cool on a cooling rack.

Mini cupcake method

1 Preheat the oven to 200°C/400°F/gas mark 6. Place the mini cupcake cases into 24-hole mini tart tins.

2 Place all the ingredients into a mixing bowl and beat together in a mixer for 2 minutes (or mix by hand) until well blended. Half-fill the cake cases with the cake mixture and level the tops.

3 Bake in the preheated oven for around 12–15 minutes, or until the cakes have risen and are firm to the touch. Remove the cakes from the tart tin and leave to cool on cooling racks.

Buttercream

Makes around 625g (1lb 6oz) of buttercream, enough for a 20.5cm (8") cake.

175g (6oz) margarine or unsalted butter, softened
450g (1lb) icing sugar, sifted
10ml (2tsp) milk
5ml (1tsp) vanilla essence

1 Put the margarine or butter in a mixer (or mix by hand) and beat until it appears lighter in colour. Add the vanilla essence and sifted icing sugar, a little at a time. Blend all the icing sugar and milk gradually until it becomes a light and fluffy mix.

2 To store, place in an airtight container and refrigerate. Use within 10 days. Bring to room temperature and mix again before use.

Cookies

175g (6oz) butter
55g (2oz) caster sugar
225g (8oz) self-raising flour, sifted
Cutters or templates
Baking trays, lightly greased
Wire cooling rack

1 Preheat the oven to 180°C/350°F/gas mark 4. Cream the butter and the caster sugar together until light and creamy. Gradually add the sifted self-raising flour, then knead together lightly.

2 Roll out the dough to a thickness of 5mm (¼") and cut out an assortment of shapes using templates or cutters. Place on the greased baking trays and bake for 8-10 minutes until pale brown. Leave to cool on a wire rack.

equipment and edibles

The checklists below are the basic 'toolkit' for all the modelling and cake covering projects throughout this book. Additional items are included at the beginning of each one if anything extra is needed, as are the specific colours and quantities of pastes. Some tools will be used far more than others but all are essential for achieving good quality results in your edible artwork.

Covering cakes

(1) Cake drums (boards) (2) Cupcake cases (3) Icing sugar shaker (4) Marzipan
(5) Non-stick board, large (6) Ribbon (7) Rolling pin, large (8) Sharp knife (9) Smoother
(10) Sugarpaste

Modelling

①　Bone tool　②　Cake cards　③　Barbeque skewers (wooden)　④　Cranked palette knife

⑤　Dresden tool　⑥　Edible glue (SK)　⑦　Food pens (SK)　⑧　Non-stick board, small

⑨　Paintbrushes: nos. 1 and 2　⑩　Rolling pin, small　⑪　Scissors　⑫　Spaghetti (raw)　⑬　Straws

⑭　Sugar Dough (SK)　⑮　White vegetable fat

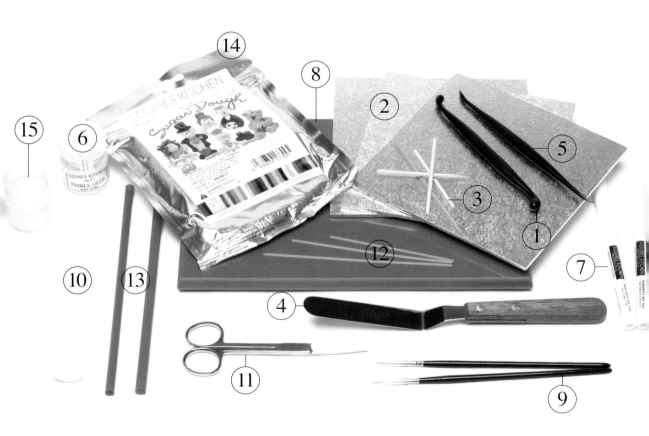

modelling basics

Sugar Dough is easy to use and is ideal for modelling animals and figures. It is available in 13 original colours and 12 natural colours, all of which can be used to create the characters in this book. I have used the original colours throughout but they can be substituted for the natural colours with very little difference. These basic hints and tips will ensure you get brilliant results every time!

- There are just a few basic shapes in modelling which can then be made into almost anything.

1 The ball: roll the paste in the middle of your hands firmly to prevent cracking.

2 The sausage: first, roll the paste into a ball then roll back and forwards on a work surface to lengthen. Roll just a little to make a short, fat sausage or continue rolling to make a longer, thinner sausage.

3 The cone: first, roll the paste into a ball. Place onto a work surface then cup your hands around the ball and turn the paste back and forth. The paste will have a flat base from sitting on the surface and the top should come to a point between your hands.

From these shapes you can make teardrops, pear shapes, discs or tapered sausages as needed for your sugar models.

● Rub a little white vegetable fat into your hands before kneading Sugar Dough: this makes it more pliable and less likely to crack, giving a more professional finish to your work. It also prevents the stronger colours from sticking to your hands when working the paste and helps to create an even consistency when adding colour to the paste.

● Wash your hands in warm, soapy water between colour changes and keep your tools clean at all times to prevent small pieces of paste from transferring onto other colours. Make sure that your hands are completely dry before handling the paste otherwise it will become sticky.

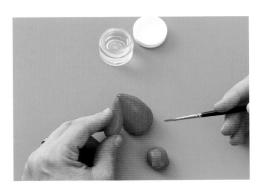

● Use SK Edible Glue to stick pieces together. Using a paintbrush, apply a little glue to the surface of the Sugar Dough before working on the next piece to allow the glue to go tacky. To stick the pieces together, hold them in position and support if necessary until they are held together securely. Working in this way should save you time.

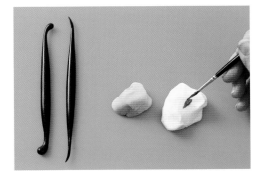

● If you would like to try working with different flavours, you can use marzipan or Cocoform (modelling chocolate) instead of Sugar Dough. Add paste food colours to create all the colours you need. As both types of paste are very soft, you may not need to use edible glue to stick pieces together.

how to model figures

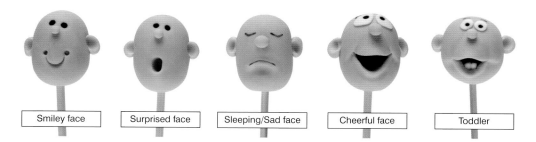

| Smiley face | Surprised face | Sleeping/Sad face | Cheerful face | Toddler |

All of the figures in this book use the same basic methods, so if you follow these you can make any character you wish, dressed appropriately in your choice of colours. Make sure you have all the basic modelling equipment to hand before you start (see page 9), plus the extra edibles listed with each example.

heads

These heads showing different facial expressions, genders and ages give a basic knowledge of how to shape a simple head through to more complex expressions with the mouth opening, teeth and a change of eyes.

Smiley face

SK Sugar Dough: 10g (¼oz) Soft Beige

SK Food Colour Pen: Black

1   Take 10g of Soft Beige Sugar Dough, pinch out a small ball for the nose and 2 slightly larger balls for the ears and set these aside.

2   Knead the remaining paste, roll into a ball and then gently shape into an oval. Push the end of a spare barbeque skewer into the base of the head and rest in the palm of your hand.

3   Push the end of a drinking straw at a 45° angle into the paste for a mouth. Push the end of a piece of raw spaghetti into the paste at both ends of the mouth for dimples.

4   Attach the smallest ball of paste with a little edible glue above the mouth for the nose.

5   Brush edible glue on either side of the head level with the nose. Take the 2 remaining small balls of paste and push the end of a bone tool (smallest end) into one side of the ball. Secure to the side of the head, smoothing the paste with the bone tool towards the front of the head.

6   For the eyes, push the end of a Black Food Colour Pen into the paste twice above the nose.

7   Once the head is complete, remove the barbeque skewer from the base and attach it to the body, securing with edible glue.

Young girl

Woman

Man

Bob with fringe

Curly hair

Surprised face

SK Sugar Dough: 10g (¼oz) Soft Beige

SK Food Colour Pen: Black

1 Follow steps 1 and 2 for the smiley face.

2 For the mouth, push the end of a paintbrush into the paste and ease it downwards a little to make an opening.

3 Complete the head following steps 4 to 7 as for the smiley face.

Sleeping/sad face

SK Sugar Dough: 10g (¼oz) Soft Beige

SK Food Colour Pen: Black

1 Follow steps 1 and 2 for the smiley face.

2 Mark the mouth with a small knife, bringing the ends of the mouth downwards. Run a bone tool underneath to emphasise the bottom lip. Smooth over the inside of the mouth with a Dresden tool.

3 Attach the nose with edible glue and run a bone tool down from the nose to each corner of the mouth. Draw the eyelids onto the head with a Black Food Colour Pen and secure the ears to the sides of the head.

Cheerful face

SK Sugar Dough: tiny amount Black, 10g (¼oz) Soft Beige, 1g (small pinch) White

SK Food Colour Pen: Black

1 Follow steps 1 and 2 for the smiley face.

2 Mark the mouth with a small knife and gently ease the paste open. Use a Dresden tool to make the opening bigger, bring the corners of the mouth upwards and mark on either side for the cheeks. Run the bone tool underneath the bottom lip and smooth over with your finger.

3 Brush a little edible glue inside the mouth opening, take a small amount of Black Sugar Dough and attach it to the back of the mouth, easing the paste into the corners with a Dresden tool.

4 Attach a small ball of paste above the mouth for the nose and 2 balls either side of the head for ears.

5 For the eyes, pinch out 2 small balls of white paste, shape into ovals, flatten and cut a straight edge at the bottom of both. Attach to the head with edible glue. Push the end of a Black Food Colour Pen into each eye for the pupils. Draw an eyebrow over each eye on the outer edge.

Toddler

SK Sugar Dough: tiny amount Black, 10g (¼oz) Soft Beige, 1g (small pinch) White

SK Food Colour Pen: Black

1   Shape the head into a ball, then make a mouth opening as for the cheerful face.

2   Add the nose, ears and white eyes (leave as small ovals) then push a Black Food Colour Pen into both eyes and draw on eyebrows above the eyes.

3   Secure a small amount of Black Sugar Dough inside the mouth opening and smooth into the corners. Roll out a tiny amount of White paste for the teeth, cut a tiny square, mark down the centre to divide the teeth and secure inside the mouth with edible glue.

Young girl

SK Sugar Dough: tiny amount Black, small amount Blue, 10g (¼oz) Soft Beige, 1g (small pinch) White

SK Food Colour Pens: Black, Red

1   Follow steps 1 and 2 of the smiley face to shape the head.

2   Mark the mouth opening and cheeks as for the cheerful face, then add the nose and ears. Secure the black paste inside the mouth opening with edible glue.

3   For the eyes, roll 2 small balls of White Sugar Dough, flatten and secure to the head above the nose. Roll 2 smaller balls of Blue Sugar Dough,

secure to the white with edible glue and push a Black Food Colour Pen into each eye. Draw on eyelashes and eyebrows with the food pen.

4   Use a Red Food Colour Pen to colour the lips, then use a damp paintbrush to even the colour out across the bottom lip.

Woman

SK Sugar Dough: tiny amount Black, small amount Brown, 10g (¼oz) Soft Beige, 1g (small pinch) White

SK Food Colour Pens: Black, Red

1   Shape the head, nose, ears and mouth as for the young girl but don't emphasise the cheeks this time.

2   Secure the Black Sugar Dough inside the mouth opening with edible glue and colour the lips with a Red Food Colour Pen, as above.

3   Gently push the end of a bone tool into the head above the nose for eye sockets. Pinch out 2 small balls of White Sugar Dough, flatten and attach inside each of the sockets with edible glue. Roll out 2 tiny balls of Brown Sugar Dough for the irises, flatten and secure to the white paste. Push the end of a Black Food Colour Pen into each eye, then use the pen to draw on the eyebrows and the eyelashes.

Man

SK Sugar Dough: 1g (small pinch) Black, 3g (just under ¼oz) Brown, 10g (¼oz) Soft Beige, 1g (small pinch) White

SK Food Colour Pen: Black

1. Make the head following the method for the cheerful face, but mark the eyebrows over the top of the eyes and not offset to one side of each eye.

2. To make the moustache, shape 2 balls of Brown Sugar Dough into teardrops and mark with a Dresden tool to resemble hair. Brush a little edible glue over the top of the upper lip and attach both pieces of paste, bringing the points of the moustache into an upwards position.

3. For the beard, shape a small ball of Brown Sugar Dough into a triangle, flatten and mark with a Dresden tool as for the moustache. Attach to the underside of the bottom lip with edible glue and bring the beard to a point.

hair

Hairstyles are as individual as faces, so try experimenting with different styles and colours. Here are a couple of examples modelled on the last 2 heads.

Bob with fringe

SK Sugar Dough: 10g (¼oz)
Yellow

1. Before you start working on the hair, brush edible glue over the head where the hair will be attached.

2. Divide 10g of Yellow Sugar Dough into 3 parts: 2g for the fringe; 3g for the side piece of hair to go behind the ear; and 5g for the back of the head.

3. Shape the last piece of paste into a flattened triangle and mark the hair with a Dresden tool. Curl the base of the hair underneath a little and secure over one ear and behind the other.

4. Shape the side piece of hair into a teardrop, flatten and mark with a Dresden tool as before. Secure to the top of the head and behind the exposed ear. Use the Dresden tool to merge the 2 pieces of paste together and hide the joins.

5. Lastly shape the fringe into a triangle and mark as before. Secure to the top of the head and merge the paste with the Dresden tool once again.

Curly hair

SK Sugar Dough: 10g (¼oz)
Brown

1. Before you start working on the hair, brush edible glue over the head where the hair will be attached.

2. You will need to make the curls and attach them to the head individually, so start at the back of the head, in the centre and at the bottom and work towards each of the ears first. Depending on the length of the hair you require, shape small amounts of paste into a teardrop shape, twist into a curl and attach to the head. Smooth down the attached piece of hair on the head with a Dresden tool.

3. Once the back of the head is covered, attach pieces of curled paste in front of each of the ears using shorter lengths of paste, then do the same at the top of the head, ending up at the crown.

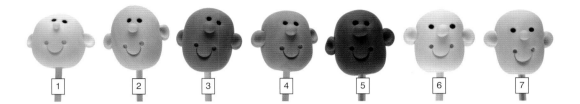

skin tone

To give your sugar figures different skin tones, use these examples as a guide to the colours you will need.

1   Equal mix of Soft Beige and White Sugar Dough

2   Soft Beige Sugar Dough

3   Teddy Bear Brown MMP

4   Equal mix of Teddy Bear Brown and White MMP

5   Teddy Bear Brown MMP with a small amount of Black Paste Food Colour added. Add more black for a darker complexion

6   Equal mix of Golden Bear Brown and White Sugar Dough

7   1 part Golden Bear Brown Sugar Dough mixed with 4 parts White Sugar Dough

feet

You can make shoes in all different styles and colours to suit your figure – these are just a few styles that I use regularly. Make the figure from the bottom up, starting with the feet, and allow plenty of time for the Sugar Dough to dry before assembling the figure so that it holds its shape.

Boots

SK Sugar Dough: 20g (¾oz) Black

1   Roll the paste into a sausage and round off both ends. Cut this in half to make 2 boots.

2   Smooth over the cut edge (top of the boot) with your fingers, then rest your finger at the front of the boot and bend the paste in half at a 90° angle.

3   Push the end of a bone tool into the top of each boot for the trousers to fit into.

Rounded shoes

SK Sugar Dough: 10g (¼oz) Brown

1   Divide the paste equally into 2 parts and roll
    each piece into a rounded oval shape.

2   Push the end of a bone tool into the paste
    towards the back of the shoe to fit either socks
    or legs into.

Pointed shoes

SK Mexican Modelling Paste (MMP): 8g (¼oz)
Teddy Bear Brown

1   Divide the paste equally into 2 parts. Roll into
    teardrop shapes and round off the pointed end.

2   Push the end of a bone tool into the paste
    towards the back of the shoes to fit the legs into.

Ballet shoes

SK Sugar Dough: 1g (small pinch)
Red, 5g (just under ¼oz) White

1   Mix the 2 colours together to
    make a soft pink colour. Divide
    the paste equally, shape into
    ovals and lengthen the toes
    between your finger and
    thumb. Square off the toe
    end on the work board.

2   Push the end of a bone
    tool into the paste at the
    back of the shoes for the legs
    to fit into.

High-heeled shoes

SK Sugar Dough: 2g (pinch) Red

1   Divide the paste in half. Shape each piece into
    a teardrop with a point at the toe end and bend
    the shoe to form an instep. Push the end of a
    bone tool into the heel end.

2   Roll a small amount of paste into a sausage
    for each heel, cut to size and attach to the
    underside of the shoe with a little edible glue.

legs

There are several different ways to make the legs
of a figure: these examples show how to make
bare legs, shorts, trousers and skirts of different
lengths. In the same way as for the body (below),
you can adjust the colour of the skin and clothing
as required.

Bare legs

SK Sugar Dough: 20g (¾oz) Soft Beige

1   Shape the paste into a sausage, leaving the
    middle slightly wider (this forms the bottom).
    Bend the paste in half and bring the ends
    together to make the legs. Cut to size if
    necessary and round off the ends to fit inside
    the socks and/or shoes.

2   Push a long barbeque skewer down through
    the top of the body and all the way down one
    leg, twisting as you push down carefully to
    avoid distorting the legs. Keep pushing the
    skewer through until it protrudes out of the leg
    by 1.5cm.

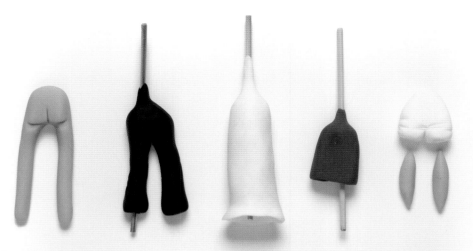

3   Mark down the centre and underneath the buttocks at the top of the legs with a Dresden tool.

Trousers

SK Sugar Dough: 30g (1oz) Black

1   Shape the paste into a sausage, making the middle slightly wider. Bend the paste in half and bring the ends together to make the legs. Cut to the required length with a sharp knife.

2   Mark creases at the tops of the legs and on either side of each leg with a Dresden tool.

3   Carefully twist and push a barbeque skewer down the body and through a trouser leg, exposing the skewer enough to fit into the shoe. Secure the top of the trousers around the skewer with edible glue.

4   Mark a light line down the centre and underneath the buttocks at the top of the trousers with a Dresden tool.

Long skirt

SK Sugar Dough: 50g (1¾oz) White

1   Shape the White Sugar Dough into a wide sausage, push your thumb into one end and pinch the paste downwards to form the base of the skirt.

2   Push and twist a barbeque skewer into the top of the skirt all the way to the base. Use edible glue to secure the skewer at the top of the skirt and pinch the paste around it.

Knee-length skirt

SK Sugar Dough: 8g (¼oz) Violet, 8g (¼oz) White

1   Mix the 2 colours together to make a mid-purple tone. Shape the paste into a wide sausage and flatten one end on the board. Push your thumb into the flattened end and pinch down the paste a little.

2   Carefully twist a barbeque skewer up through the skirt. Secure the skewer at the top of the skirt with edible glue and pinch the paste around the skewer.

Shorts

SK Sugar Dough: 4g (just under ¼oz) Soft Beige, 15g (½oz) White

1   Divide the Soft Beige Sugar Dough in half. Make 2 sausage shapes and roll each end into a point. Push a length of barbeque skewer down through the middle of a leg.

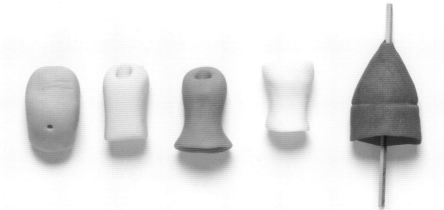

2   Shape the White Sugar Dough into a cone, flatten slightly and make a 0.5cm long incision at the base to form 2 legs in the shorts. Smooth over the cut edges.

3   Mark creases at the top of the legs with a Dresden tool.

4   Push the end of a paintbrush into the base of the shorts for the legs to fit into, then push a spare barbeque skewer through the top of the shorts and out of one leg and remove.

5   Push the leg with the barbeque skewer through the hole just made in the shorts. Secure the leg to the base of the shorts with edible glue and pinch the paste at the top of the shorts around the skewer to secure it in place. Secure the second leg into the other hole in the shorts.

6   Mark the front of the shorts with the blunt side of a small, sharp knife. Mark a light line down the centre and underneath the buttocks at the back of the shorts with a Dresden tool.

bodies

There are several different ways to make the body of a figure, depending on what they are wearing. I have listed the colours of Sugar Dough used in the examples shown but you can, of course, change the colours of the skin tone and clothing to personalise your models.

Man's torso

SK Sugar Dough: 25g (just over ¾oz) Soft Beige

1   Shape the Sugar Dough into a wide sausage. Make the top of the body/shoulders slightly slimmer than the middle (tummy) and round off the shoulders.

2   Shape the lower end of the body so it is slightly thinner than the middle, push your thumb into the underside and pinch down the paste to fit over the top of the lower body/legs neatly.

3   Push a spare barbeque skewer down the centre of the body using a twisting motion so as not to distort the paste. Remove this then secure the body over the skewer protruding from the legs using edible glue. Smooth over any joins for a neat finish. Push the end of a paintbrush into the middle of the tummy for a tummy button.

Leotard

SK Sugar Dough: 1g (small pinch) Red, 15g (½oz) White

1   Mix a small pinch of Red Sugar Dough into the White to make a soft pink colour. Shape into a sausage, flatten one end on the board and push the end of a bone tool into the top for a neck opening.

2 Push a spare barbeque skewer down through the centre from the top with a twisting motion, then remove the skewer.

3 Secure the body over the barbeque skewer in the legs of the figure using edible glue.

Jumper (female)

SK Sugar Dough: 15g (½oz) Golden Bear Brown

1 Shape the Sugar Dough into a sausage and flatten one end of the paste on the board. Push your thumb into the flat underside and pinch the edges of the paste down to fit over the trousers/skirt.

2 Push the end of a bone tool into the top for a neck opening and nip in the waistline between your fingers and thumb to help to form a bust.

3 Push a spare barbeque skewer down through the centre of the top with a twisting motion, remove and secure over the barbeque skewer in the legs using edible glue.

Bodice

SK Sugar Dough: 15g (½oz) White

1 Shape the Sugar Dough into a wide sausage, push your thumb into the underside of one end and pinch the paste down between your finger and thumb (this will fit over the skirt of the wedding dress snugly).

2 At the other end of the bodice, i.e. the top, repeat the same process but go a little deeper into the paste. This part will hold the shoulders at the top of the body. Smooth around the middle of the bodice to bring in the waistline a little and mark down the back of the bodice

from top to bottom with the blunt edge of a small, sharp knife.

3 Use a Dresden tool to mark the corset eyelets on either side of the vertical line down the back from top to bottom.

4 Push a spare barbeque skewer down through the middle of the bodice, twisting as you go through the paste. Remove this skewer then secure the bodice in place over the barbeque skewer protruding from the top of the skirt with edible glue.

Coat/shirt

SK Sugar Dough: 40g (1½oz) Red

1 Shape the Red Sugar Dough into a cone. Push your thumb into the underside of the wide end and pinch the paste down around the edges so that the join of the trousers will be covered neatly.

2 Mark the front of the coat from the top to the bottom with the blunt edge of a small, sharp knife. Mark creases around the middle of the jacket using a Dresden tool.

3 Push a spare barbeque skewer down through the middle of the coat with a twisting motion, remove and then secure over the barbeque skewer in the trousers with a little edible glue.

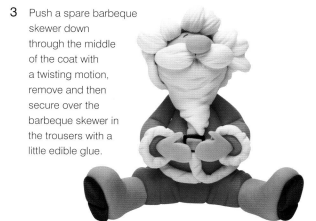

arms and hands

The arms you make will also depend on what the figure is wearing: if the arms are bare you can make the arms and hands all-in-one, if the person is wearing clothes with sleeves you can make sleeves to match the body and add the hands separately.

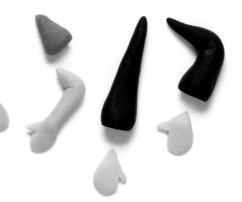

Bare arms

SK Sugar Dough: 10g (¼oz) Soft Beige

1 Roll the Sugar Dough into a long sausage. Pinch each end between your finger and thumb to form a paddle and then make an incision with a small, sharp knife on one side of each end to create the thumbs.

2 Ease out each thumb a little and smooth over the cut edges with your fingers.

3 Separate the arms by making 2 diagonal cuts for the shoulders in the middle of the paste. Mark the elbows with a Dresden tool and bend slightly.

4 Secure the arms to the top of the body with a little edible glue.

Short sleeves

SK Sugar Dough: 4g (just under ¼oz) in the same colour as the body

1 Divide the paste equally into 2 pieces and shape each into a cone.

2 Push the end of a paintbrush into the larger end of both sleeves to secure the arms into.

3 Make the arms and hands in the same way as for bare arms but cut the arms just above the elbow and shape to a point to fit inside the sleeves.

Long sleeves

SK Sugar Dough: 15g (½oz) in the same colour as the body

1 Roll the paste into a sausage and bring the ends to a rounded point. Cut in half with a small, sharp knife to make 2 arms of equal length. Smooth over the cut area with your fingers.

2 Mark the elbow with a Dresden tool and bend. Push the end of a paintbrush into the paste at the wrist of both arms to fit the hands into (see below).

Hands

SK Sugar Dough: 2g (pinch) Soft Beige

1 Divide the paste in half so you have 1g per hand. Roll each piece into a ball, shape into a teardrop and pinch between your finger and thumb to flatten slightly.

2 Use a small, sharp knife to make an incision on one side of the paste, ease out a little to form the thumb and smooth over the cut edge with your fingers. Secure to the inside of the cuff of each sleeve with edible glue.

Whether you're making a cake for a colleague, friend or relative, what we do for a living makes a great subject matter for cake-top figures. By looking at their uniform you can have great fun tailoring each figure to suit the recipient!

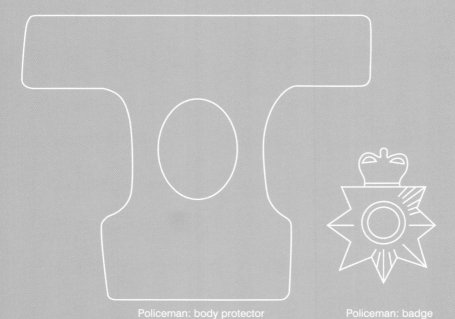

Policeman: body protector

Policeman: badge

OCCUPATIONS

builder

edibles

SK Sugar Dough: 19g (¾oz) Black, 40g (1½oz) Blue, 30g (1oz) Golden Bear Brown, 32g (1oz) Soft Beige, 2g (pinch) White, 8g (¼oz) Yellow

SK Mexican Modelling Paste (MMP): 24g (¾oz) Teddy Bear Brown

SK Food Colour Pen: Red

equipment

14cm (5½") wooden barbeque skewer

Important note: Remember to remove the wooden skewer before the model is eaten.

1 Divide the Soft Beige Sugar Dough as follows: 10g for the belly; 1g for the neck; 6g for the arms; and 15g for the head.

2 Divide the Black Sugar Dough as follows: 12g for the shoes and 6g for the hair.

3 Divide the Teddy Bear Brown MMP as follows: 20g for the t-shirt and 2 x 2g for the sleeves.

4 Divide the paste for the shoes in half and shape into ovals.

5 To make the blue jeans, follow the instructions to make trousers on page 18 using Blue Sugar Dough. Once made, leave for as long as possible to firm.

6 Roll the belly into a ball and then flatten into a disc to fit over the top of the jeans. Secure over the skewer with a little edible glue and mark the belly button at the front with the end of a paintbrush. Mark the buttocks with the blunt side of a small knife at the back of the figure.

7 Shape the t-shirt into a cone, push your thumb into the underside of the cone and pinch down edge of the paste. Push a spare skewer into the middle of the t-shirt and remove. Attach the t-shirt to the jeans by brushing a little edible glue over the top of the jeans and securing the t-shirt over the barbeque skewer. Mark creases around the sides of the t-shirt using a Dresden tool.

8 Shape each sleeve into a cone and push the end of a paintbrush into the base of each one for the arms to be attached to. Secure the sleeves to either side of the t-shirt using edible glue then mark with a Dresden tool.

9 Divide the paste for the neck into 2 and roll into 2 balls, one slightly smaller than the other. Take the larger ball and secure to the top of the t-shirt over the skewer with a little edible glue. Secure the smaller ball on top of this.

10 Roll the paste for the arms into a sausage shape. Gently flatten both ends between your finger and thumb and make a small incision on side of each hand with a small, sharp knife. Ease out the thumb and smooth over the cut edges. Cut the sausage in half and shape the cut ends into a point which can be fitted inside the t-shirt sleeves. Mark the elbow of each arm with a Dresden tool and bend slightly. Secure into place with edible glue and bring the hands to the front of the body with the palms facing upwards, ready for the bricks to be affixed.

11 For the bricks, roll out the Golden Bear Brown Sugar Dough to a thickness of 0.5cm and cut out approximately 11 bricks measuring 1.5cm x 2cm in size. Mark the top in the middle of each one with a bone tool. Glue a stack of six together, leave one loose and glue the remaining four into the builder's arms.

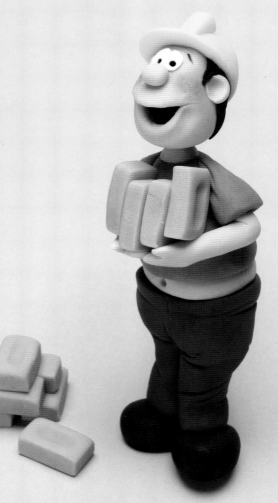

builder cupcakes

Hardhat

You will need 4g (just under ½oz) of Yellow Sugar Dough to make the hat. Reserve 2 small balls for the brim and the front peak of the hat. Shape the remaining paste into a ball and flatten the base on a board. Take one of the reserved balls, shape into a wedge and attach to the front of the hat with edible glue. Roll the remaining ball into a sausage, flatten and cut a straight edge on one side bringing each end to a point. Secure to the front of the hat with edible glue.

Bricks

Divide 10g (¼oz) of Golden Bear Brown Sugar Dough into 3 equal parts and shape into rectangles. Indent the centre of all the bricks using a bone tool.

Lunch break

To make the newspaper and sandwich you will need 6g (just under ¼oz) of White Sugar Dough, 2g (pinch) of Golden Bear Brown and 1g (small pinch) of Red. Roll the White paste into a fat sausage, flatten and mark an opening on 3 sides of the newspaper with a Dresden tool. Write on the name of the newspaper using a Red Food Colour Pen and draw on some lines for text using a Black Food Colour Pen. Roll out the Golden Bear Brown Paste, cut 2 rectangles the same size and set aside. Make the filling from the Red paste slightly larger than the rectangles and mark the sides with a Dresden tool. Secure inside the 2 rectangles with edible glue and cut out teeth marks with a small, sharp knife. Attach the sandwich to one side of the newspaper.

12 Follow the steps on page 13 to make a head with a cheerful face. Colour the builder's cheeks with a Red Food Colour Pen then brush over them with a slightly damp brush in order to blend the colour into the face.

13 Roll the hair into a ball, flatten into a disc and then mark with a Dresden tool. Brush the back of the head and in front of the ears with a little edible glue and attach the hair to the head. Smooth the hair onto the head with a Dresden tool and bring the paste around to the front of the ears.

14 To make the builder's hardhat, divide the Yellow Sugar Dough into 2g and 6g pieces. Roll the larger amount into a ball, push your thumb in underneath and pinch down the paste to form a dome. Divide the remaining yellow paste in half, shape one into a pyramid shape, cut to size and secure to the front of the hat. Roll the remaining paste into a sausage and flatten one edge with your fingers. Cut a straight edge on the wider side and attach to the front of the hat with edible glue.

policeman

edibles

SK Sugar Dough: 105g (3¾oz) Black, 19g (¾oz) Soft Beige, 50g (1¾oz) White,

SK Food Colour Pens: Red, Black

equipment

14cm (5½") wooden barbeque skewer

Body protector template (see page 22)

Important note: Remember to remove the wooden skewer before the model is eaten.

1 Divide the Black Sugar Dough as follows: 50g for the trousers; 12g for the shoes; 2g for the tie; 20g for the body protector; 2g for the belt; 6g for the belt tools; 12g for the helmet; and 1g for the finishing touches of the body protector.

2 Divide the White Sugar Dough as follows: 30g for the shirt; 12g for the sleeves; 1g for the collar; 2g for the hair; 3g for the body protector; keep the remaining paste for finishing touches.

3 Divide the Soft Beige Sugar Dough as follows; 1g for the neck; 8g for the arms; and 10g for the head.

4 Divide the paste for the shoes into 2 equal pieces and shape into ovals.

5 Follow the instructions on page 18 to make the trousers then attach both of the shoes to the trousers with edible glue and leave to dry.

6 For the shirt, shape the White Sugar Dough into a cone, push your thumb in underneath and pinch down the paste to fit over the trousers. Push a skewer through the middle, remove and secure to the top of the skewer in the trousers using edible glue.

7 Roll a ball for the neck, flatten slightly and push a skewer through the centre. Remove the skewer and secure the neck to the top of the shirt with edible glue.

8 To make the tie, pinch out a small amount of paste and shape into a triangle for the knot. Roll out the remaining paste, cut a strip for the lower part of the tie and secure to the shirt with edible glue. Attach the triangular knot at the top over the strip.

9 For the body protector, roll out the paste and use a small, sharp knife to cut out the shape using the template. Smooth over the cut edges with your fingers and secure to the shirt. Cut to size if necessary and smooth over the joins at the sides.

10 Roll the Sugar Dough for the belt into a sausage, press it flat and cut 2 straight edges 0.5cm wide with a sharp knife. Brush edible glue around the top of the trousers and secure the belt in place, starting at the front and leaving an overlap of 0.5cm for the buckle. Cut to size and secure the overlap. Mark the other side of the buckle with the blunt side of a small knife.

11 Roll the sleeves into a sausage, cut in half and push the end of a paintbrush into the cut end for the arms to be attached into. Run the blunt edge of a small knife around each of the sleeves for a cuff and secure the sleeves into the inside of the body protector using edible glue. Mark the gathered creases at the top of the sleeves with a Dresden tool and position the sleeves towards the back of the body.

12 For the collar, roll the Sugar Dough into a sausage, flatten and cut a strip 0.5cm wide to fit around the neck. Cut the front ends of the collar at an angle and secure into place using edible glue.

13 Make the arms following the instructions for short sleeves on page 21. Mark the elbows with a Dresden tool and bend slightly. Secure into the sleeves with edible glue and bring the hands together at the back on top of each other.

14 Follow the instructions for the cheerful face on page 13 but add some teeth at the top and bottom of the mouth. To make the teeth, roll out

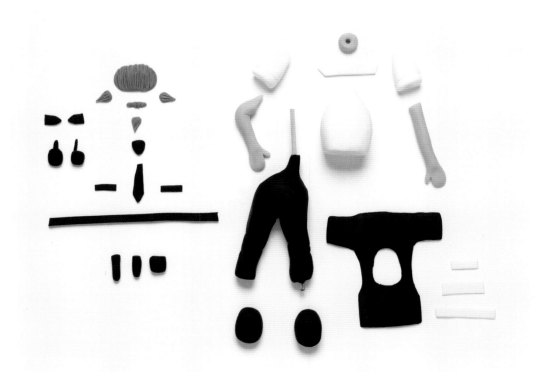

a small ball of white paste and cut 2 small strips the length of the lips. Mark the teeth with the blunt edge of a small knife, brush edible glue inside the top and bottom lip and secure the teeth into position, starting with the bottom set first, and cut to size if necessary. Use a Red Food Colour Pen to colour his cheeks and brush over the colour with a slightly damp brush to blend the colour into the face.

15 To make the policeman's hair, mix the White Sugar Dough with a tiny amount of Black to make a grey colour. Brush a little edible glue on the chin, over the top lip, in front of the ears and on the back of the head ready for the hair to be attached. Pinch out a small sausage for the moustache, flatten and mark with a Dresden tool then fix into position. Pinch out a small triangle for the beard, mark with a Dresden tool and fix to the chin. Pinch out 2 small triangles for the hair in front of the ears, mark with a Dresden tool and secure to the head. Shape the remaining paste into a flattened oval, mark with a Dresden tool and secure to the back of the head, merging the paste towards the triangles at the front.

16 For the finishing touches on the body protector, roll out the Black Sugar Dough and cut 2 small strips 0.5cm wide. On both, cut one end into a point and secure at the shoulders using edible glue, tucking one under the collar and one slightly over the collar. Roll out another 1g of the Black Sugar Dough and cut 2 strips slightly smaller in width and 1.5cm long for the pockets. Secure them to the front of the protector. Pinch a small ball of black paste for the radio, square it off, mark with the pointed end of a Dresden tool and secure to the front shoulder of the protector with edible glue. Roll a tiny sausage of Black Sugar Dough, cut to 0.5cm and attach to the top of the radio.

17 Roll out 3g of White Sugar Dough and cut 3 labels as follows: one across the back from shoulder to shoulder 0.5cm wide, marked with a Blue Food Colour Pen for a chequered effect; one slightly wider but just shorter than the first with 'POLICE' written on it with a Blue Food Colour Pen; and the third 0.5cm wide x 1.5cm long with 'POLICE' written on it in Black Food Colour Pen for the front of the body protector. Secure all 3 in place onto the protector with edible glue.

18 For the belt tools, divide up the paste into 4 parts, make 2 squares and 2 tubes with a small, sharp knife and attach to the belt with edible glue.

19 To make the policeman's helmet, use 8g of the Black Sugar Dough for the main part of the helmet, 3g for the peak of the helmet and the remainder for the ridge. Shape the larger ball into a cone with a smooth top. Roll the small ball of Sugar Dough into a ball, flatten between your finger and thumb and bring one end out to a point for the front of the helmet. Secure the main part of the helmet on top of the disc with edible glue. Use the remaining black paste to form the ridge from the top of the helmet down the back, roll into a sausage, square it off and secure with edible glue. Pinch a small ball of white paste for the top of the helmet, divide into 2 with one piece smaller than the other and secure both on top with edible glue. Roll out a small ball of White Sugar Dough and cut out a police badge. Use a small, sharp knife to make the markings and secure to the front of the helmet.

policeman cupcakes

Walkie talkie

Take 10g (¼oz) of Black Sugar Dough and reserve a small ball. Shape the remaining paste into a rectangle, make 12 indentations with the end of a paintbrush for the speaker and indent a line at the bottom with the blunt edge of a knife. Roll the reserved piece of paste into a sausage, cut to size and secure to the top of the walkie talkie with edible glue.

Police badge

Mix 6g (just over ¼oz) of White Sugar Dough with a small amount of Black to make grey. Roll out and cut out a badge from the template, then mark all around the badge and the crown on top with the blunt edge of a small, sharp knife. Roll 1g (small pinch) of Blue Sugar Dough into a ball, flatten between your finger and thumb and secure to the centre of the badge with edible glue. Write on the word 'POLICE' using a Black Food Colour Pen.

Blue light

Roll 2g (pinch) of Black Sugar Dough into a ball and then pinch between your finger and thumb to form a disc. Shape 10g (¼oz) of Blue Sugar Dough into a dome and secure on top of the black disc with edible glue.

fireman

edibles

SK Sugar Dough: 85g (2¾oz) Black, 2g (pinch)
Blue, 5g (just under ¼oz) Golden Bear Brown,
20g (¾oz) Red, 12g (just over ¼oz) Soft Beige,
5g (just under ¼oz) White, 9g (¼oz) Yellow

SK Food Colour Pens: Black, Blue, Red

equipment

12.5cm (5") wooden barbeque skewer

Important note: Remember to remove the
wooden skewer before the model is eaten.

1 Divide the Black Sugar Dough as follows: 12g
for the shoes; 30g for the trousers; 30g for the
jacket; 12g for the sleeves; and 1g for the neck.

2 Divide the Soft Beige as follows: 2g for the
hands and 10g for the head.

3 Divide the Sugar Dough for the shoes into 2
equal pieces and shape into ovals.

4 To make the fireman's trousers, follow the
instructions on page 18.

5 For the jacket, follow the instructions for
making a coat on page 20 (the same as for
Father Christmas but in Black Sugar Dough). Roll
the neck into a ball, flatten to make a disc and
secure over the skewer to the top of the jacket with
edible glue.

6 Make the sleeves from Black Sugar Dough
following the steps for long sleeves on page
21. Brush edible glue on either side of the top of
the jacket, secure the arms in place and mark the
tops of the shoulders with a Dresden tool.

7 Use 4g of the White Sugar Dough to make the stripes on the jacket. Roll the paste out and cut strips which are 0.5cm wide. Make these as follows: 1 to fit around the base of his jacket; 4 x 1.5cm long strips for the base of the trousers; 2 x 2.5cm long strips for the end of the sleeves; a 2cm strip across the back, between the shoulders; and 2.5cm and 0.5cm long strips for the top of the jacket. Attach these in place using edible glue.

8 To make the torch, use 1g of the Yellow Sugar Dough, pinch out a small ball and shape the rest into a tube. Secure to the front of the jacket with edible glue, push the end of a bone tool into the reserved ball and attach to the top of the tube. Roll out a small ball of Black Sugar Dough, cut a strip to wrap around the tube and secure with edible glue.

9 For the hosepipe, roll the Red Sugar Dough into a long sausage and wrap it around the base of the fireman's feet and up to the front of his jacket. Secure onto the jacket with a little edible glue.

10 To make the nozzle of the hosepipe, mix 1g of White Sugar Dough with a tiny amount of Black Sugar Dough to make grey. Pinch out a tiny ball, shape the remaining paste into a cone and secure to the end of the hosepipe with edible glue. Brush a little glue at the end of the cone, push the end of a paintbrush into the tiny ball and secure to the end of the cone.

11 Make the hands by following the instructions on page 21. Secure them in place with a little edible glue so that they hold the hosepipe.

12 Roll the pinch of Blue Sugar Dough into a teardrop, brush edible glue into the end of the nozzle and secure the drip in place.

13 Make the head by following the steps for the surprised face (page 13). Add colour to the cheeks with a Red Food Colour Pen and brush over with a slightly damp paintbrush to merge the colour into the skin.

14 Use the Golden Bear Brown Sugar Dough to make the hair. Use 3g for the back: shape it into an oval, mark with a Dresden tool and secure to the back of the head with edible glue. Divide the remaining paste in 2 for the sideburns, shape into rectangles, mark with a Dresden tool and secure in place.

fireman cupcakes

Fire hose

Roll 7g (just under ¼oz) of Red Sugar Dough into a sausage, cut one end straight and curl around into a small pile. Take 1g (small pinch) of Black Sugar Dough, shape into a small cone and attach to the cut edge of the red hose with edible glue. Pinch a tiny ball of Black paste, push the end of a paintbrush into the centre and secure to the end to complete the nozzle. Shape a small amount of Blue Sugar Dough into a teardrop and secure to the end of the nozzle.

Bucket of water

Mix 8g (¼oz) of White Sugar Dough with a tiny amount of Black to make grey. Reserve a small ball for the handle. Shape the rest of the paste into a sausage shape with flattened ends, push the end of a bone tool into one end of the paste and work the paste at the top of the bucket, gradually working towards the centre. Roll the reserved paste into a thin sausage, brush edible glue on either side of the bucket and secure the length of paste in place, cutting to size if necessary. Push the end of a paintbrush into the paste where the handles join. Roll 2g (pinch) of Blue Sugar Dough into a ball, flatten between your finger and thumb and secure to the inside of the bucket with edible glue.

15 For the main part of the helmet, take 6g of the Yellow Sugar Dough, roll into a ball and flatten on a flat surface. Push your thumb into the underside and pinch down the paste a little around the edges to create a lip. Secure to the top of the head with edible glue. Roll out the remaining paste into a sausage, flatten on one side and cut a straight edge on the thicker side. Attach to the back of the helmet. Repeat the same process again but this time make the peak of the helmet thinner. Gather the trimmings, knead together and roll into a sausage. Pinch the paste to form a ridge and attach to the top of the helmet, leaving space for the badge at the front.

16 Make the fireman's badge with a pinch of White Sugar Dough: roll it into a ball, flatten and attach to the front of the helmet. Mark with Black and Blue Food Colour Pens.

nurse

edibles

SK Sugar Dough: 10g (¼oz) Black, 31g (just over 1oz) Blue, 7g (¼oz) Golden Bear Brown, 16g (½oz) Soft Beige, 22g (¾oz) White

equipment

12.5cm (5") wooden barbeque skewer

Important note: Remember to remove the wooden skewer before the model is eaten.

1 Divide the Soft Beige Sugar Dough as follows: 5g for the arms; 10g for the head; and 1g for the neck.

2 Divide the Black Sugar Dough into 2 equal pieces and shape into ovals for the shoes.

3 Use 30g of the Blue Sugar Dough and follow the instructions on page 18 for making trousers. Once made, make an incision with a sharp knife on one side of the trousers for a pocket and leave to dry.

4 To make the tunic, mix 20g of White Sugar Dough with the remaining Blue Sugar Dough to make a pale blue paste. Reserve 6g for sleeves, lapels and collar. Shape the remaining paste into a cone, push your thumb into the underside and pinch the paste down to fit over the trousers. Nip in the waistline and form a bust then run a bone tool underneath to emphasise the shape. Make 2 small incisions on either side of the tunic, then mark down the centre with the blunt edge of a knife for the opening at the front. Use a Dresden tool to make the creases around the middle. Push a bone

tool into the paste at the neck then push a spare skewer into the centre, remove and secure the tunic over the skewered trousers with edible glue.

5 Divide the neck into 2 uneven balls. Model the larger one into an oval for the neck opening in the tunic and the smaller one into a disc for the neck. Secure both into place over the skewer.

6 For the sleeves use 4g of the pale blue divided in half. Shape each piece into a cone and push the end of a paintbrush into the flat end where the arms will be secured. Brush edible glue on either side of the tunic and attach the sleeves in place. Mark the shoulders with a Dresden tool.

7 To make the lapels and collar, roll out the remaining pale blue Sugar Dough. Cut 2 triangles for the lapels and secure to the front of the tunic, overlapping each other, with edible glue.

Knead together the remaining paste again, roll out and cut a strip for the collar. Round off the ends and secure around the neck with edible glue.

8 Trim the collar and the sleeves with a small amount of White Sugar Dough rolled out into a thin sausage, glue into place and cut to size.

9 To make the watch, roll out the remaining White Sugar Dough and cut a small strip 0.5cm wide x 0.2cm deep. Attach to the front of the tunic by the collar. Roll a small ball of white paste and push the end of a bone tool into the centre for the watch face, then attach to the underside of the small strip.

10 Use the White Sugar Dough trimmings to make the name label. Roll out the paste, cut a rectangular shape 1cm x 0.5cm and secure to the base of the tunic with edible glue. Roll a tiny sausage of White Sugar Dough and secure to the centre of the rectangle. Mark squiggles on the name label with a Black Food Colour Pen.

11 Follow the instructions for making the arms with short sleeves (see page 21). Cut the hand off one of the arms and attach it inside the pocket opening in the trousers. Secure the other to the front of the tunic with edible glue.

12 Follow the instructions on page 12 to make a basic head with a smiley face.

13 To make the nurse's hair, divide the Golden Bear Brown Sugar Dough as follows: 3g for the back of the head; 2 triangles for in front of the ears; 1g for a ponytail; and the remaining paste for the fringe. Shape the hair for the back of the head into an oval, mark with a Dresden tool and secure with edible glue. Mark the 2 triangles with a Dresden tool and secure in place in front of the ears. Shape the ponytail into a teardrop, mark with a Dresden tool as before and secure to the base of the head with edible glue. Use the remaining paste for the fringe: make teardrop shapes, mark with a Dresden tool and secure to the head, leaving a parting to one side.

14 For the bow, use 1g of the Blue Sugar Dough. Pinch out a small ball for the centre and divide the rest in half. Shape 2 triangles and secure them to the back of the head over the ponytail, then mark with a Dresden tool. Roll the small ball into a tiny sausage shape and place in the centre of the 2 triangles, tucking the ends in at the top and bottom with a Dresden tool.

nurse cupcake

Roll out 3g (large pinch) of Red Sugar Dough and cut a cross shape using a small, sharp knife.

astronaut

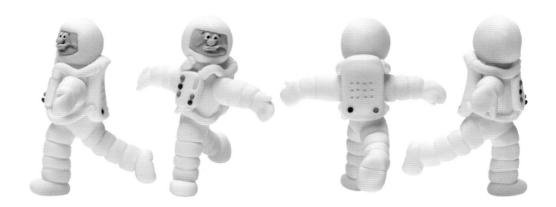

edibles

SK Sugar Dough: 2g (pinch) Blue, 2g (pinch) Red, 3g (small ball) Soft Beige, 153g (5¼oz) White, 2g (pinch) Yellow

equipment

2 wooden barbeque skewers: approximately 11.5cm (4½") long and 9cm (3½") long

Important note: Remember to remove the wooden skewer before the model is eaten.

1 Divide the White Sugar Dough as follows: 12g for the boots; 40g for the trousers; 20g for the body; 2g for the neck; 2 x 12g for the arms; 30g for the helmet; 4g for the front pack; 15g for the backpack; and 5g for the pipes. Reserve a pinch of the White Sugar Dough for the eyeballs.

2 Divide the paste for the boots in half and shape into 2 ovals.

3 Roll the trouser paste into a sausage, bend the legs around and mark the creases all around the legs with a Dresden tool to make sections on the suit. Push the longer length of barbeque skewer through one of the legs and into one of the boots, then secure with edible glue. Pinch the paste around the top of the trousers to hold to the barbeque skewer in place.

4 Bend the other leg upwards and support with food-grade sponge pieces or rolled up kitchen towel. Secure the second boot to the end of the leg with edible glue. Leave this to dry for as long as possible, preferably overnight.

5 Roll the body into a fat sausage and push your thumb into one end in order to pinch the edge of the paste down a little to fit over the trousers. Push a spare barbeque skewer through the body, remove and then secure over the trousers and skewer using edible glue.

6 Roll the neck into a ball and pinch between your finger and thumb to form a disc. Using edible glue, secure the neck to the body over the skewer.

7 Push the smaller barbeque skewer through the body horizontally in order to support the arms, carefully avoiding the central skewer. Roll each arm into a sausage and gently flatten one end between your finger and thumb. Make an incision on one side of the hand with a sharp knife for a thumb. Ease the thumb out a little and smooth over the cut edges. Mark around the wrist with a Dresden tool and mark a 2 more rings further up the arms. Secure to the body over the skewer with edible glue. Repeat for the second arm, making sure that the thumbs are facing the right way round.

8 Shape the front pack into a rectangle measuring 2cm x 2.5cm and secure to the front of the body using a little edible glue. Mark the holes for the buttons with the end of a piece of dried spaghetti or a barbeque skewer.

9 Roll the helmet into a ball and mark the visor with the edge of a small knife. Push the end of a bone tool into the paste inside the marked area, cut away any excess paste from the middle and smooth over. Push the end of a spare barbeque skewer into the base of the helmet, remove and secure over the skewer at the neck with edible glue.

10 To make the face, roll out the Soft Beige Sugar Dough and cut a shape to fit inside the helmet visor and secure it with a little edible

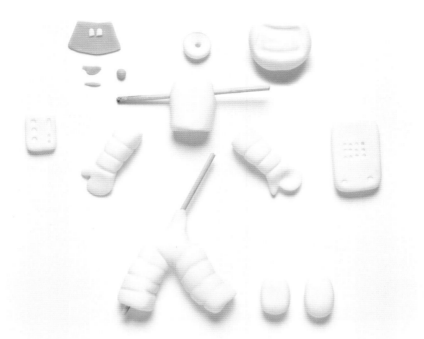

glue. Pinch out a small piece of paste, roll into a tiny sausage and secure to the face for the bottom lip. Brush over with a glue brush (no glue) to blend the edges into the paste. Pinch out a second piece of paste for the top lip, bend into shape and secure over the bottom lip. Blend in as before. Use the brush to form the cheeks, gently easing the paste until it forms the shape of the face. Roll out a small ball of paste for the nose and secure above the lips.

11 For the eyes, pinch out 2 small balls from the White Sugar Dough reserved earlier, flatten and attach above the nose. Push the end of a Black Food Colour Pen into each of the eyes for the pupils.

12 Roll the backpack into a rectangular shape measuring 3.5cm x 4.3cm. Secure to the back of the body using edible glue. Again, mark the holes for the buttons with the end of a piece of dried spaghetti or a barbeque skewer.

13 Roll the pipes into sausages long enough for one to come from the front pack to the backpack, another to come from the helmet to the backpack, and 2 smaller pipes to connect at the base of the front and backpacks. Secure in place with edible glue. Run a Dresden tool around each end to look like a connecting join.

14 For the buttons, make small balls of Red and Blue Sugar Dough and stripes of Yellow Sugar Dough. Using edible glue, secure into the grooves on the front and backpacks.

astronaut cupcake

To make the rocket you will need 10g (¼oz) of Blue Sugar Dough and 8g (¼oz) of Red. Shape the Blue paste into a sausage and bring one end to a point for the top of the rocket. Run your fingers down either side of the sausage to shape the rocket. Divide the Red paste in half and shape each piece into a teardrop. Cut the top of each at an angle to fit on either side of the rocket and secure with edible glue.

vicar

edibles

SK Sugar Dough: 70g (2½oz) Black, 70g (2½oz) White

SK Mexican Modelling Paste (MMP): 15g (½oz) Teddy Bear Brown

SK Food Colour Pen: Black

equipment

14cm (5½") wooden barbeque skewer

Important note: Remember to remove the wooden skewer before the model is eaten.

1 Divide the Black Sugar Dough as follows: 12g for the shoes; 40g for the cassock; 1g for the top of the cassock; less than 1g for the collar; 10g for the scarf; tiny amount for the hair; and 3g for the bible.

2 Divide the White Sugar Dough as follows: 40g for the surplice; 1g for the collar; 20g for the sleeves; tiny amount for the teeth; 3g for the hair; and 4g for the bible.

3 To make the shoes, split 12g of Black Sugar Dough in half and make 2 ovals. (Do not push a bone tool into paste for this outfit.)

4 Roll the Black Sugar Dough for the cassock into a short, wide sausage. Push your thumb into the paste at one end and pinch the edge of the paste downwards between your finger and thumb, pinching more around the area that will sit over the shoes. Push a barbeque skewer through the middle with a twisting motion, secure to the top of the cassock using edible glue and pinch the paste around the skewer. Ease the cassock over the shoes and attach them to the underside with

downward strokes around the neck area to resemble gathered material. Cut a straight edge across the top of the neck and leave to dry.

7 For the top of cassock, roll 1g of Black Sugar Dough into a ball and push a spare skewer into the centre. Remove the skewer then secure the ball over the skewer at the neck and onto the surplice with edible glue.

8 Roll a tiny ball of Teddy Bear Brown MMP, push over the skewer at the neck and secure to the black paste with edible glue.

9 To make the collar, roll out 1g of White Sugar Dough into a strip. Cut a rectangle to fit around the neck, attach at the back of the neck, cut to size and secure the ends in place. Roll out another strip using a tiny piece of Black Sugar Dough, cut another rectangle slightly smaller than before and secure to the white collar, leaving the front exposed to show the white collar underneath.

10 For the sleeves, roll 20g of White Sugar Dough into a sausage and taper the ends to a rounded point. Cut through the centre to make 2 equal arms. Push your thumb into the cut end of each piece and pinch down the paste to open up the sleeves. March each elbow with a Dresden tool, bend and secure to the top of the body, bringing the sleeves round to the front.

11 Roll the paste for the scarf into a long sausage and flatten with a rolling pin. Cut the edges straight, making the scarf 1cm wide. Brush a little edible glue around the back of the neck and shoulders and rest the scarf centrally around the neck. Secure to the front of the surplice and cut to size at the bottom with a pair of scissors.

12 Secure the sleeves over the top of the scarf. Knead together the trimmings of Black Sugar Dough from the scarf and pinch out 2 x 1g pieces for the cuffs inside the cassock. Brush

edible glue. Leave to dry for as long as possible, preferably overnight.

5 Shape 40g of White Sugar Dough into a cone for the surplice. Push your thumb into the underside and pinch down the paste all around the edge, making sure that there is a large enough hole underneath to fit the surplice over the cassock. Push a spare barbeque skewer up through the centre of the surplice and remove. Push the end of a paintbrush into the hole to make a bigger opening so that the base fits over the paste of the cassock around the skewer. Brush edible glue around the skewer and ease the surplice over the skewer.

6 Run a bone tool up and down the gown to make pleats. Using a Dresden tool, make

edible glue inside each of the sleeve openings. Shape the 2 balls of black paste into cones and push the end of a paintbrush into the wider end of each one. Secure inside each of the sleeves. Leave to dry before attaching the head and hands to the figure.

13 Using 1g of Teddy Bear Brown for each hand, follow the steps on page 21. Secure to the inside of the black cuffs in the sleeves with edible glue, cupping the hands together.

14 Make the head from 10g of Teddy Bear Brown MMP, following the instructions for the cheerful face on page 13. Add a top set of teeth inside the mouth by rolling out a small ball of White Sugar Dough and cutting a strip the length of the top lip. Mark the teeth with the blunt edge of a small knife, brush edible glue inside the top lip and secure the teeth into position. Mark some wrinkles on the forehead and on either side of the nose carefully with a Dresden tool.

15 Mix together a pinch of Black Sugar Dough with 3g of White to make grey. Brush edible glue over the back of the head and in front of the ears. Pinch out 2 small balls of paste to go in front of the ears, then shape the remaining paste into a disc, mark the hair with a Dresden tool and secure to the back of the head. Make 2 triangles from the remaining pieces of grey paste, mark with a Dresden tool and secure to the head in front of the ears. Merge the hair paste together using a Dresden tool.

16 To make the pages of the bible, roll out 4g of White Sugar Dough and cut a 2.5cm x 2cm rectangle. Mark down the centre with the blunt side of a knife. For the bible cover, roll out 3g of Black Sugar Dough, secure the white pages on top of the black paste and cut around the outside. Leave to dry before drawing lines onto the pages with a Black Food Colour Pen. Secure to the hands, resting on the sleeves for support.

vicar cupcake

You will need 15g (½oz) of White Sugar Dough and 10g (¼oz) of Black. Shape the White paste into a rectangle and set aside. Roll out the Black paste and cut a larger rectangle to cover the White paste like a book, then secure with edible glue. Mix a little cooled, boiled water with SK Antique Gold Metallic Lustre Dust and, using a no.1 paintbrush, carefully paint a cross onto the front cover of the bible.

We all have a favourite hobby, from playing sport to dancing or hitting the slopes! No matter what age the recipient is or what they love doing, you can replicate it in sugar.

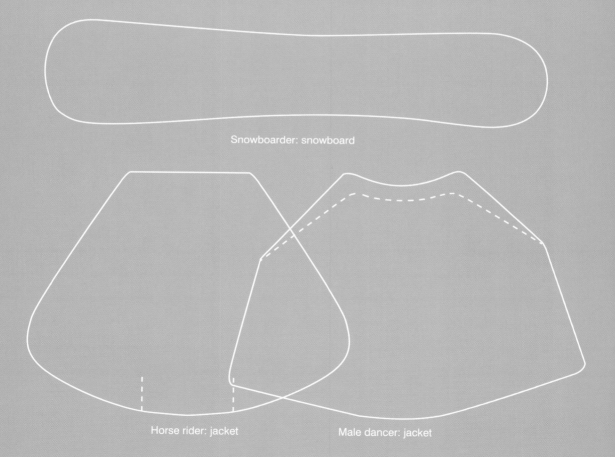

Snowboarder: snowboard

Horse rider: jacket

Male dancer: jacket

HOBBIES

horse rider

edibles

SK Sugar Dough: 30g (1oz) Black, 5g (just under ¼oz) Brown, 15g (½oz) Golden Bear Brown, 13g (just under ½oz) Soft Beige, 2g (pinch) White

SK Mexican Modelling Paste (MMP): 20g (¾oz) Cream Celebration, 30g (1oz) Teddy Bear Brown

SK Food Colour Pens: Black, Red

equipment

Jacket template (see page 44)

14cm (5½") long wooden barbeque skewer

9cm (3½") length of dried spaghetti

Important note: Remember to remove the wooden skewer before the model is eaten.

1 Divide the Black Sugar Dough as follows: 20g for the boots; 8g for the hat; and 2g for the whip handle.

2 Divide the Soft Beige Sugar Dough as follows: 10g for the head; 1g for the neck; and 2g for the hands.

3 For the whip colour the spaghetti piece with the Black Food Colour Pen. Dip one end of the spaghetti into edible glue and work a small ball of Black Sugar Dough down one end for a handle. Take another small ball of black paste, roll into a sausage, flatten, bend over to form a loop and secure to the other end. Set aside to dry.

4 To make the riding boots, follow the instructions on page 16.

5 Use the Cream Celebration MMP to make the jodhpurs. Shape the paste into a tapered sausage with a wide middle and bring the legs together. Push the skewer into the top of the jodhpurs, down through one of the legs and into one of the boots. Secure the other leg into the top of the boot with edible glue and mark creases at the top and at the back of the jodhpurs with a Dresden tool. Pinch the paste at the top of the jodhpurs around the skewer to secure and leave to dry.

6 For the jumper shape the Golden Bear Brown Sugar Dough into a cone, push your thumb into the paste and pinch the edge of the paste down to fit over the jodhpurs. Push a spare skewer through the centre, remove and secure to the skewered jodhpurs with edible glue. Nip in the waistline to form a bust and push a bone tool into the neck area.

7 Divide the neck into 2 uneven balls and use the larger one to fit inside the top of the jumper, attaching with edible glue. Flatten the other ball into a disc and secure over the top of the skewer onto the jumper insert.

8 To make the jacket, roll out the Teddy Bear Brown MMP and cut out the shape for the main jacket using the template. Curl back the paste at the collar and cut 2 incisions at the back. Glue the jacket to the body and overlap it at the front. Cut 2 small rectangles for the pockets and secure in place. Cut 2 long triangles for the lapels and secure to the front opening. Make 3 small buttons for the front of the jacket and 2 smaller ones for the back. Attach with edible glue and push the end of a paintbrush into the centre of each.

9 For the arms, knead together the remaining paste, roll into a sausage and taper the ends to rounded points. Cut down the centre. Mark the elbows with a Dresden tool and bend each arm at the elbow, then push the end of a paintbrush into the cut end for the hands to be attached into later. Secure the arms to the jacket with edible glue, bringing both arms to the back of the jacket. Mark the top of each shoulder with a Dresden tool.

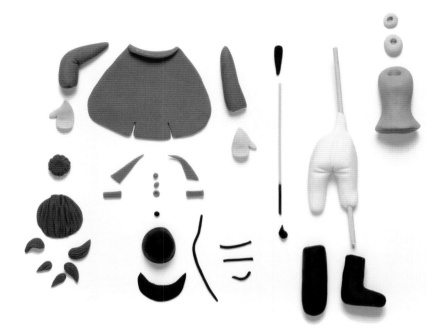

10 Follow the instructions on page 21 to make the hands and secure inside the jacket sleeves. Bring the fingers upwards and attach the whip inside the hands with edible glue. Ease the hands over the whip carefully.

11 Follow the steps on page 12 to make a basic smiley head but make the nose pointed instead of a small ball. Make the eyes in the same way as for the young girl on page 14 and draw on the lipstick with a Red Food Colour Pen.

12 For the hair, divide the Brown Sugar Dough as follows: 2g for the back of the head; 2 small triangles to go in front of the ears; 1g for the bun; and any remaining paste for the front of the head. Shape the hair for the back into an oval, mark with a Dresden tool and secure to the back of the head at the base with edible glue. Mark the 2 triangles for the front of the ears with a Dresden tool and secure in place. Roll the bun into a ball, pinch into a disc, mark with a Dresden tool and attach to the base of the hair with edible

glue. Use the remaining brown paste to make teardrop shapes at the front of the head, mark with a Dresden tool and secure in place with edible glue.

13 When making the riding hat, use 4g of the Black Sugar Dough for the main part of the hat. Shape this into a ball and flatten on the work surface to form a dome. Push your thumb into the underside and pinch down the paste a little around the edge. Secure to the top of the head with edible glue.

14 Roll 2g of Black Sugar Dough into a sausage, flatten on one side and cut a straight edge on the other. Secure the thicker edge to the front of the hat for a peak. Roll out the remaining paste into a long, thin sausage, attach to the hat behind the ears and under the chin and cut to size. Attach 2 smaller lengths in front of the ears from the hat to the chin strap. Cut another small length and attach to the strap under the chin with edible glue.

horse rider cupcakes

Horseshoe

Mix 6g (just under ¼oz) of White Sugar Dough with a pinch of Black paste to make a grey colour. Roll into a sausage, flatten and bend around to make a horseshoe shape. Pinch the front of the horseshoe to lift the paste up a little and mark four holes on either side with a Dresden tool.

Rosette

To make the rosette you will need 15g (½oz) of Red Sugar Dough and a small ball of Yellow. Roll out the red paste, cut out 2 ribbons, then cut an inverted 'V' out of the bottom of both and rest one on top of the other. Knead together the trimmings and divide into 2 balls, one slightly smaller than the other, then flatten both. Mark around the outer edge of each circle with a Dresden tool, secure the smaller circle onto the larger one and then attach both over the top of the ribbons with edible glue. Roll the Yellow Sugar Dough into a ball, flatten and secure to the centre of the rosette with edible glue. Draw a '1st' in the centre of the yellow paste using a Black Food Colour Pen.

ballerina

edibles

SK Sugar Dough: 8g (¼oz) Brown, 2g (pinch) Red, 43g (1½oz) Soft Beige, 63g (2¼oz) White

SK Food Colour Pen: Black

equipment

7.5cm (3") long wooden barbeque skewer

5cm (2") circle cutter

Veining tool (optional)

Important note: Remember to remove the wooden skewer before the model is eaten.

1 Divide the Soft Beige Sugar Dough as follows: 20g for the legs; 1g for the neck; 10g for the arms; and 12g for the head.

2 Divide the White Sugar Dough as follows: 8g for the ballet shoes; 30g for the petticoat; 10g for the tutu; and 15g for the body.

3 Roll the legs into a sausage and taper the ends so that it is thicker in middle. When both ends are long and thin and are the same length and size, bring the legs around to meet each other and cross one over the other.

4 For the ballet shoes, mix the White Sugar Dough with a tiny amount of Red to make a pale pink colour. Use 5g of this mixture to make the shoes following the instructions on page 17. Secure the legs inside each of the shoes with edible glue. Roll out the remaining paste and cut a small strip to wrap around the ankles for the ribbons. Cut to size and secure in place with edible glue.

5 Roll out the White Sugar Dough for the petticoat and cut out 3 circles using the circle cutter. Frill around the edge of each circle with either a veining tool or the end of a paintbrush and secure over the top of the legs with edible glue.

6 Mix the Sugar Dough for the tutu with a little Red Sugar Dough to make a pale pink which matches the ballet shoes. Roll out the paste, cut out a circle and frill as before using either a veining tool or paintbrush. Secure over the top of the petticoats then insert a wooden skewer through the skirts using a twisting motion. Leave to dry.

7 To make the leotard, follow the instructions on page 20.

8 Divide the paste for the neck in 2, roll both pieces into balls and skewer the centre of each. Leave the skewer in one of these balls and then use this skewer to pierce the body and secure the neck onto the ballerina's top. Brush over the neck with a little edible glue and then ease the second ball onto the skewer.

9 Follow the instructions on page 21 to make the ballerina's arms and hands. Glue in place at the shoulders and rest the hands on top of each other at the front of the tutu.

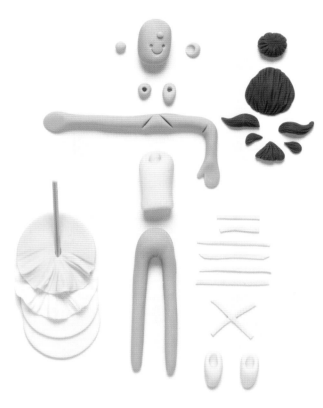

10 To make the head for the ballerina, follow the instructions on page 12 for the basic smiley face. Push the end of a Black Food Colour Pen into each of the eyes for the pupils.

11 For the hair, use 3g of the Brown Sugar Dough for the back of the head. Roll into a ball, flatten and mark with a Dresden tool. Brush over the head with edible glue, attach the back piece of hair and smooth it into the head with a Dresden tool. Make 2 small triangles of paste, mark with a Dresden tool and secure in front of the ears. Smooth the paste into the hair at the back to hide the joins.

12 Use 2g of Brown Sugar Dough for the bun at the back of the head, roll into a ball and pinch between your finger and thumb a little. Mark all around the edges with a Dresden tool and secure to the hair near the back of the neck. Divide the remaining paste into 3, shape one piece into a triangle, flatten slightly and mark all over with a Dresden tool. Secure to the front of the head for the fringe. Shape the 2 remaining pieces of paste into teardrop shapes, mark as before and bend the ends up a little. Secure to the head on either side of the fringe.

ballet cupcakes

To make the ballet shoes, mix 10g (¼oz) of White Sugar Dough with a small amount of Red to make a soft pink paste. Divide the paste into 3 equally, then follow the instructions on page 17 to make the shoes. Use the remaining paste to make 2 pairs of ribbons and secure to the back of the shoes with edible glue.

footballer

edibles

SK Sugar Dough: 12g (just under ½oz) Black, 32g (just over 1oz) Blue, 6g (just under ¼oz) Golden Bear Brown, 17g (just over ½oz) Soft Beige, 24g (just over ¾oz) White

SK Food Colour Pen: Black

equipment

11.5cm (4½") long wooden barbeque skewer

Important note: Remember to remove the wooden skewer before the model is eaten.

1 Divide the Blue Sugar Dough as follows: 2g for the socks; 18g for the shirt; and 12g for the arms.

2 Divide the Soft Beige Sugar Dough as follows: 4g for the legs; 1g for the neck; 2g for the hands; and 10g for the head.

3 Divide the White Sugar Dough as follows: 8g for the football; 15g for the shorts; and 1g for the shirt.

4 Roll the paste for the football into a ball and leave to dry. When completely dry, draw on the pattern using a Black Food Colour Pen.

5 Make the shoes from Black Sugar Dough following the instructions on page 17 for rounded shoes.

6 Divide the paste for the socks into 2 unequal balls and shape each piece into a cone. Push the end of a paintbrush into the top of each one and secure the pointed end inside the shoes with edible glue. Mark creases on each one with a Dresden tool.

7 To make the footballer's legs and shorts, use the measured White and Soft Beige Sugar Dough and follow the instructions on page 19. Leave to dry.

8 For the shirt, shape the Blue Sugar Dough into a cone, push your thumb into the base and pinch the paste downwards around the edge. Make an indent at the top of the cone for the inset at the neck using a bone tool. Push a spare skewer through the centre, remove and secure the shirt to the top of the shorts over the skewer using edible glue. Shape the White Sugar Dough for the top of the shirt into a triangle and push it over the skewer, securing in place with edible glue.

9 Roll the paste for the neck into a ball and flatten into a disc. Secure to the top of the shirt over the skewer using edible glue.

10 Follow the instructions on page 21 to make long sleeves and hands. Bring the hands together at the front with the palms facing upwards.

11 Follow the instructions on page 12 to make a basic head but instead of adding a smile, use a knife to make an incision at an angle. Push a piece of dried spaghetti into the corner of the mouth and use a bone tool to lift the bottom lip and the cheek.

12 For the hair, use 3g of the Golden Bear Brown Sugar Dough for the back of the head. Shape into an oval, mark with a Dresden tool and secure to the back of the head with edible glue. Model 2 small triangles for the hair in front of the ears, mark with a Dresden tool and secure in place. Use the remaining Sugar Dough for the top of the head, roll into a ball and flatten the hair that will be at the back between your finger and thumb. Mark with a Dresden tool across the front and then stipple all across the top and secure to the top of the head. Smooth over any joins to merge the hair.

13 Secure the ball into the footballer's hands with edible glue.

football cupcake

Roll 10g (¼oz) of White Sugar Dough into a ball and then flatten one side on a board, keeping the top rounded. Mark the ball pattern with a Black Food Colour Pen.

rugby player

edibles

SK Sugar Dough: 12g (½oz) Black, 17g (just over ½oz) Soft Beige, 53g (1¾oz) White, 8g (¼oz) Yellow

SK Food Colour Pens: Black, Blue, Red

equipment

11.5cm (4½") long wooden barbeque skewer

Important note: Remember to remove the wooden skewer before the model is eaten.

1 Follow the same instructions for making the footballer on pages 53 to 55 using the quantity of pastes below. You will only need to make a few changes as follows: omit the inset in the neck of the shirt; leave one arm straight; keep the mouth smiley; and change the hairstyle as described below.

2 Make the shoes from 12g of Black Sugar Dough and the socks from 2g of White.

3 For the legs and shorts, use 15g of White and 4g of Soft Beige Sugar Dough.

4 For the shirt, you will need 18g of White Sugar Dough.

5 Use 1g of Soft Beige Sugar Dough for the neck.

6 Make the arms from 12g of White Sugar Dough and the hands from 2g of Soft Beige.

7 To make the head, use 10g of Soft Beige Sugar Dough and follow the instructions on page 12 to make a smiley face.

8 For the hair you will need 8g of Yellow Sugar Dough. Brush edible glue over the head where the hair to be attached. Use 3g for the back of the head, shape into an oval, mark with a Dresden tool and attach in place. Pinch out 2 triangles for the fronts of the ears, mark as before and attach. Build up the top with teardrop-shaped pieces of paste, mark with a Dresden tool and attach to the centre of the head. The teardrops should get progressively smaller as you reach the top.

9 To make the ball, roll 6g of White Sugar Dough into an egg shape, set aside and leave to dry. When completely dry, draw on a pattern using Red and Blue Food Colour Pens. When dry, secure the ball to the hand using edible glue.

rugby cupcake

Roll 10g (¼oz) of Golden Bear Brown Sugar Dough into a sausage and bring each end to a rounded point. Flatten the base on a board but retain the shape of the ball on top. Mark a line across the centre with the edge of a blunt knife then indent either side of the line with the end of a paintbrush.

yoga workout

edibles

SK Sugar Dough: 67g (2¼oz) Black, 8g (¼oz)
Golden Bear Brown, 10g (¼oz) Red, 30g (1oz)
Soft Beige, 60g (2oz) Violet, 10g (¼oz) White

SK Food Colour Pens: Black, Red

equipment

9cm (3½") long wooden barbeque skewer

Important note: Remember to remove the
wooden skewer before the model is eaten.

1 To make the yoga mat, roll out 60g of Violet
Sugar Dough and cut a rectangle measuring
15cm x 7.5cm. Set aside to dry.

2 Reserve 2g of Black Sugar Dough for the belt
then use the remaining paste to make the
leggings. Roll the paste into a sausage with a much
larger middle for the body then mark creases across
the buttocks, knees and thighs with a Dresden tool.
Bend one leg in front of the body and bring the other
up behind the body. Push the end of a paintbrush
into the ends of both legs to fit the feet into.

3 Divide the Soft Beige Sugar Dough as follows:
6g for the feet; 2g for the bust and neck; 10g for
the arms; and 12g for the head.

4 For the feet, divide the Soft Beige Sugar Dough
into 2 equal pieces and shape each one into a
foot and ankle. Secure each one into the openings
in the leggings with edible glue.

5 Reserve a tiny piece of White Sugar Dough for
the eyes. To make the vest, mix together the
remaining White and Red Sugar Dough to make a
pink colour. Shape into a cone, push your thumb

into the underside and pinch down the paste around the edge. Bend the top back slightly and push a bone tool into the neck opening to widen it a little. Run the bone tool around the back to make creases under the bust. Secure the top over the leggings with edible glue.

6 Roll the reserved 2g of Black Sugar Dough into a sausage, flatten with a small rolling pin and cut a strip 0.5cm wide for a belt. Secure around the vest with edible glue, cut to size and mark with the blunt edge of a small, sharp knife.

7 Shape the Soft Beige Sugar Dough for the bust into a teardrop and mark with the blunt edge of a small, sharp knife. Secure inside the opening at the top of the vest with edible glue. Pinch a small ball of paste for the neck, then push a wooden skewer through the neck and down through the body to help support the head. Leave to dry for a few hours, preferably overnight.

8 To make the arms, follow the instructions on page 21 for bare arms. Secure the right arm down the body and rest it on the right thigh. Bend the left arm back to hold onto the toes of the left foot, mark under the armpit with a bone tool and secure in place with edible glue.

9 Take the paste for the head and pinch out a tiny ball for the nose and 2 balls for the ears. Shape the head into an oval, push the end of a spare wooden skewer into the base and remove. Shape the mouth by pushing the end of a paintbrush into the head, then run a bone tool around the outside of the mouth gently to push the lips out. Run a bone tool around the cheek area to lift the cheeks out and make 2 indents for the eye sockets. Attach the nose in place.

10 Secure the head over the skewer in the figure with edible glue. Brush a little glue on either side of the head, push the end of a bone tool

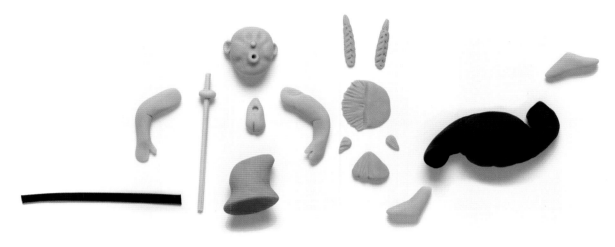

into each of the ears and attach to the sides of the head, smoothing in any joins.

11 Make the eyes from the reserved White Sugar Dough and secure inside the sockets. Push the end of a Black Food Colour Pen inside each of the eyes and draw on eyelashes and eyebrows. Use a Red Food Colour Pen to colour up the cheeks and lips. Brush over with a barely damp paintbrush to disperse the red colour.

12 Before making the hair from Golden Bear Brown Sugar Dough, brush over the head with edible glue. Use 3g for the back of the head, roll into a ball, flatten and mark a parting down the centre with the blunt edge of a small, sharp knife. Mark either side of the central line with a Dresden tool and secure to the back of the head. Smooth the ends into the head for a neat finish.

13 Pinch 2 small triangles of paste for the hair in front of the ears, mark as before and secure in place. Smooth the paste into the hair at the back of the head to hide the joins. Make another triangle from 2g of paste, flatten slightly and mark with a Dresden tool. Secure to the top of the head and smooth over the joins with a Dresden tool.

14 For the plaits use 1g for each, roll into a sausage and bring one end down to a point. Mark 0.5cm from the end with a Dresden tool for a hair band and mark alternate diagonal

lines with a Dresden tool. Secure to the back of the hair and down the back.

15 Lastly, secure the figure to the yoga mat using edible glue.

yoga cupcakes

Yoga mat

To make the mat you will need 18g (just under ¾oz) of Violet Sugar Dough. Roll out 5g of the paste and cut a rectangle measuring 4cm x 2cm (1½" x ¾"). Knead together the trimmings with the remaining paste and shape into a sausage the same length as the rectangle. Flatten the ends on a board and mark a swirl on both ends with the blunt edge of a small knife. Secure the roll of paste to one edge of the rectangle with edible glue.

Sweat bands

Divide 4g (just under ¼oz) of Violet Sugar Dough in half and roll each piece into a ball. Flatten slightly between your finger and thumb, push the end of a paintbrush into the centre and push against the paste to make the hole larger. Smooth over the edges with your finger where the paintbrush has pushed the paste out.

snowboarder

edibles

SK Sugar Dough: 3g (small ball) Black, 34g
(1¼oz) Blue, 12g (just under ½oz) Brown, 40g
(1½oz) Golden Bear Brown, 30g (1oz) Red, 12g
(just under ½oz) Soft Beige, 2g (pinch) White,
10g (¼oz) Yellow

equipment

14cm (5½") and 6.5cm (2½") long wooden
barbeque skewers

Snowboard template (see page 44)

Important note: Remember to remove the
wooden skewer before the model is eaten.

1   Divide the Red Sugar Dough as follows: 20g
    for the snowboard; 2g for the scarf; and 8g for
the hat.

2   Roll out the Red Sugar Dough for the
    snowboard and cut out the shape from the
template. Smooth around the edges with your
fingers and gently lift up the front and back of the
board. Leave to dry.

3   Divide the Brown Sugar Dough in half and
    shape into ovals for the boots.

4   To make the bindings, roll out 3g of Black Sugar
    Dough and cut 4 strips, each 0.5cm wide, to fit
over the top of the boots. Secure to the boots with
edible glue and tuck the ends underneath.

5   Make the trousers from 40g of Golden Bear
    Brown Sugar Dough following the instructions
on page 18. Make the base of the trousers quite
wide. Push the skewer into the boot, then into the
snowboard and secure them together with edible
glue. Attach the other boot to the snowboard
behind the front leg and secure the trousers in
place. Leave to dry.

6 Shape 20g of Blue Sugar Dough into a cone, push your thumb into the underside and pinch the edge of the paste down to fit over the trousers. Push a spare skewer through the centre, remove and secure the body over the skewered trousers with edible glue. Mark creases on the sides with a Dresden tool. Roll out 2g of Blue Sugar Dough for the pocket, cut a 2cm square and attach to the front of the jacket with edible glue.

7 Make the sleeves from 12g of Blue Sugar Dough following the instructions on page 21. Attach the right arm to the side of the jacket. Insert the shorter piece of skewer down the length of the arm, leaving room at the wrist end for the hand to be attached inside later. Push the skewer into the top of the jacket at an angle as if the figure is waving.

8 Shape 2g of Blue Sugar Dough into a triangle for the hood, push a bone tool into one end and ease out the paste, holding onto the point of

the hood so it doesn't become misshapen. Bring the ends of the hood up, secure to the back of the jacket with edible glue and smooth the ends into the top of the jacket. Push the end of a paintbrush into the front of the jacket 3 times for buttons.

9 For the scarf, shape 2g of Red Sugar Dough into a triangle, mark with a Dresden tool and ease over the skewer to secure to the top of the jacket.

10 Make the hands from 2g of Soft Beige Sugar Dough following the instructions on page 21.

11 Make the head from 10g of Soft Beige Sugar Dough following the instructions on page 13 for the cheerful face but using the eyes shown on the baby head.

12 For the hair you will need 10g of Yellow Sugar Dough. Brush edible glue over the

head where the hair will be attached. Make small sections of hair in triangular shapes and mark with a Dresden tool. Attach the hair, starting at the back of the head and working around the ears. Add a second layer at the back and front, finishing off with the fringe (don't fold the fringe back until the hat is in place). Lift the ends of the hair slightly to create movement.

13 Take the Red Sugar Dough reserved for the hat and reserve 3 balls for the tassels. Shape the remaining paste into a cone, push your thumb into the underneath and pinch down the paste a little. Shape the top of the cone into a triangle by pulling out the paste slightly and mark the gathers with a Dresden tool. Mark the edge of the hat with the edge of a small knife for the ribbed area and secure to the head with edible glue. Fold back the fringe pieces over the edge of the hat. Make 3 tassels from the reserved paste, mark with a small knife then indent the base of each one with a Dresden tool. Brush edible glue on each point of the hat and secure the tassels in place.

snowboarder cupcake

You will need 10g (¼oz) of Black Sugar Dough to make a pair of goggles. Roll out the paste and cut a strip 0.3cm (⅛") wide x 5cm (2") long and set aside. Knead together the trimmings and shape into a rectangle. Indent the top and bottom centrally with a Dresden tool then push a bone tool into each section to create an indentation. Attach the strip of paste to each side of the goggles with edible glue and push the end of a Dresden tool into the attached ends twice to secure the strap in place.

ballroom dancers

edibles

Female dancer

SK Sugar Dough: 10g (¼oz) Golden Bear Brown, 38g (1¼oz) Soft Beige, 96g (3¼oz) White

SK Food Colour Pen: Red

Male dancer

SK Sugar Dough: 68g (just over 2¼oz) Black, 8g (¼oz) Brown, 15g (½oz) Soft Beige, 16g (½oz) White

equipment

Female dancer

12.5cm (5") long wooden barbeque skewer

Male dancer

Jacket template (see page 44)

14cm (5½") long wooden barbeque skewer

Important note: Remember to remove the wooden skewer before the model is eaten.

Female dancer

1 Divide the Soft Beige Sugar Dough as follows: 15g for the legs; 2g for the shoulders; 1g for the neck; 10g for the arms; and 10g for the head.

2 Divide the White Sugar Dough as follows: 2g for the shoes; 12g for the bodice; 80g for the skirt; and 2g for the belt.

3 To make the legs, follow the instructions on page 17 for making bare legs but keep them straight and leave to dry.

4 For the dancer's shoes, follow the instructions on page 17 for pointed, high-heeled shoes and attach to the end of each leg with edible glue.

5 Make the bodice by following the instructions on page 20. Attach this to the top of the legs.

6 Shape the shoulders into an oval, push the end of a spare skewer through the centre, remove the skewer and secure inside the top of the bodice with edible glue.

7 Roll the neck into a ball, flatten slightly and secure over the skewer to the top of the shoulders with edible glue.

8 Build up the skirt in layers and support each layer with either rolled up kitchen towel or food-grade sponge pieces. Roll out the paste and cut 7.5cm x 5.5cm sections, working on one at a time. Cover the remaining piece to prevent it from drying out. Mark each section of paste with the edge of a paintbrush to give a gathered effect, pinch the paste together at the top and attach to the bodice with edible glue. Mark around the top of each section into the bodice with a Dresden tool for more gathers. Continue to work all around the bodice for a first layer, lifting up the skirt at the base for movement and leave to dry. Repeat the same process to create a second layer and place rolled pieces of kitchen towel between the layers to lift them up, giving more movement in the skirt.

9 Roll out the White Sugar Dough for the belt and cut a strip that is wider in the centre to go around the base of the bodice over the top of the skirt. Attach to the bodice with edible glue, overlapping the ends at the front, and cut to size if necessary.

Note: If you are making the dancing couple, this is the point to bring the male dancer together with the female dancer to connect them with the arms.

10 To make the arms, follow the instructions on page 21 to make bare arms. Secure one of the hands to the hand of the male dancer and rest the other on his shoulder. Leave to dry.

11 Make the dancer's head by following the instructions for the smiley face on page 12. Draw on lipstick with a Red Food Colour Pen.

12 Before making the hair, brush edible glue over the head where the hair will be attached. Use 5g of the Golden Bear Brown Sugar Dough for the back of the head, shape into a flattened oval, mark with a Dresden tool and attach in place. Using 2g of the Golden Bear Brown Sugar Dough for each of the side pieces of hair, shape into flattened teardrops, mark with a Dresden tool and attach to the head. Swing the hair outwards and smooth over any joins with a Dresden tool.

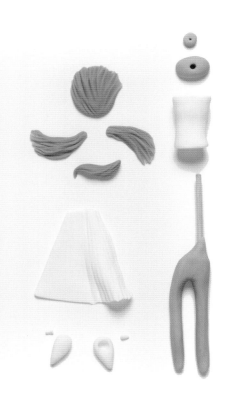

Use the remaining paste for the fringe, shape into a teardrop and mark with a Dresden tool. Secure over the top of the hair towards one side.

Male dancer

1 Divide the Black Sugar Dough as follows: 12g for the shoes; 30g for the trousers; 1g for the bowtie; 15g for the jacket; and 10g for the sleeves.

2 Divide the Soft Beige Sugar Dough as follows: 1g for the neck; 2g for the hands; and 12g for the head.

3 To make the shoes, divide the Black Sugar Dough in half and shape each piece into an oval.

4 Make the trousers by following the instructions on page 18. Leave to dry.

5 Use 15g of the White Sugar Dough to make the shirt. Shape into a cone, push a spare skewer into the centre, remove and secure the shirt over the top of the skewered trousers with edible glue.

6 Roll the neck into a ball, flatten and secure over the skewer to the top of the shirt with edible glue.

7 Use the remaining White Sugar Dough to make the shirt collar. Roll the paste into a sausage, flatten and cut 2 straight edges 0.5cm wide. Wrap around the neck, cut the ends at an angle and secure in place with edible glue.

8 For the bowtie, pinch a small ball out of the Black Sugar Dough and divide the remaining paste into 2 triangles. Mark the triangles with a Dresden tool and secure to the top of the shirt with edible glue. Flatten the small ball of paste and secure to the centre of the triangles with edible glue, tucking the ends in with a Dresden tool.

9 To make the jacket, roll out the Black Sugar Dough and cut out the jacket shape using the template. Smooth over the cut edges with your fingers, secure to the body and fold back the collar and lapels. Overlap the front of the jacket and attach 3 tiny balls for buttons, then push the end of a paintbrush into the centre of each.

Note: If you are making the female dancer to go with the man, this is the point to bring the 2 figures together.

10 Follow the instructions on page 21 to make the sleeves and attach to either side of the jacket with edible glue. Rest one arm on a large piece of rolled up kitchen towel or food-grade sponges and the other around the waist of the lady dancer. Leave to dry.

11 Follow the steps on page 21 to make the hands. Attach one to the waist area and the other to the hand of the lady dancer.

12 Follow the instructions on page 12 to make a basic smiley head.

13 For the hair divide the Brown Sugar Dough as follows: 3g for the back of the head; 2 small triangles for in front of the ears; and the rest for the top of the head. Shape the hair for the back of the head into a flattened oval, mark with a Dresden tool and secure to the head with edible glue. Mark the triangles with a Dresden tool, attach in front of the ears and smooth down the paste towards the back of the head. Use the remaining paste for the top of the head, roll into a ball and pinch between your finger and thumb on one side to form a wedge. Mark with a Dresden tool and secure to the head. Smooth the paste into the hair at the back of the head.

dancing shoes cupcakes

Make a pair of pointed, high-heeled shoes from 7g (just under ¼oz) of Red Sugar Dough following the steps on page 17. Dust the shoes with SK Magic Sparkles Metallic Lustre Dust.

Make a pair of rounded shoes from 10g (¼oz) of Black Sugar Dough following the steps on page 17.

cub scout

edibles

SK Sugar Dough: 2g (pinch) Blue, 8g (¼oz)
Black, 3g (small ball) Brown, 3g (small ball)
Golden Bear Brown, 26g (just under 1oz) Green,
3g (small ball) Red, 16g (½oz) Soft Beige, 16g
(½oz) White

equipment

2 x 11.5cm (4½") and 1 x 6.5cm (2½") long
wooden barbeque skewers

Important note: Remember to remove the
wooden skewer before the model is eaten.

1 Divide the Soft Beige Sugar Dough as follows:
4g for the legs; 10g for the head; and 2g for
the hands.

2 Divide the White Sugar Dough as follows: 12g
for the shorts and 4g for the scarf.

3 To make the shoes, divide the Black Sugar
Dough in half and roll into 2 ovals. Push the
end of a bone tool into the paste for the socks to
fit into later.

4 Divide the Brown Sugar Dough unevenly into
2 to create one sock which is longer than the
other. Roll each piece into a cone shape, push the
handle of a paintbrush into the centre of both and
mark with a Dresden tool for the creases. Secure
the socks inside the indents of the shoes with a
little edible glue.

5 Divide the paste for the legs unevenly into 2
and shape each into a sausage with a point
at both ends. Brush a little edible glue into each of
the socks and secure a leg into each sock. Push a
wooden skewer through one leg and into the shoe
and leave to dry.

6 For the shorts, mix the White Sugar Dough with a small pinch of Black Sugar Dough to make a grey colour. Shape the paste into a cone, flatten the base and cut with a small knife. Round off the cut edges with your fingers and mark with a Dresden tool.

7 Push the end of a paintbrush into the base of each leg. Push a spare skewer through one leg of the shorts, remove and secure the leg with the skewer into the shorts with edible glue. Secure the second leg and mark the front of the shorts with the blunt edge of a knife for the zip. Pinch the paste around the skewer at the top of the shorts.

8 Mix the Green Sugar Dough with a little Black Sugar Dough to make a darker green colour. Divide this as follows: 10g for the body; 10g for the arms; and 6g for the cap.

9 Shape the body into a cone, push your thumb into the underside and pinch down the paste. Ease a spare skewer up through the body, remove and then attach to the shorts with a little edible glue, securing the body over the skewer. Use a Dresden tool to mark around the base of the shirt.

10 Follow the instructions on page 21 to make the sleeves. Once made, secure to the body and mark the shoulders with a Dresden tool.

11 Make the hands following the instructions on page 21. Push the smaller skewer into the palm of one of the hands and secure with edible glue.

12 For the neck, roll a small ball of Soft Beige Sugar Dough and secure to the top over the skewer with a little edible glue.

13 To make the scarf, mix the White Sugar Dough with a little Blue in order to make a pale blue colour. Roll this out fairly thinly. Next, take 2g of Red Sugar Dough and roll out until it is the same thickness as the blue. Cut stripes of the red and place onto the blue, then roll over once more to blend the pastes. Cut out a triangle for the back of the scarf and glue to the back of the neck with a little edible glue. Cut a further 2 strips of the blue and red paste at an angle 0.5cm wide and roll them into tubes. Bend one tube in half and attach to the front of the neck with edible glue. Cut the other tube to size so that it fits around the neck

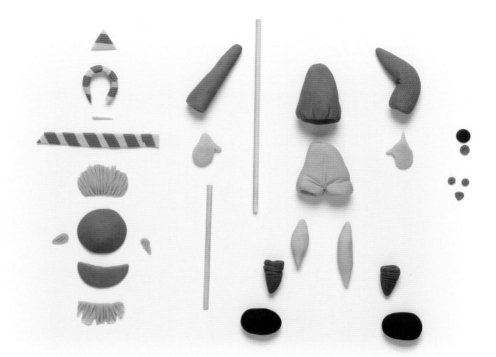

and glue in position. Roll a tiny amount of the pale blue paste into a tiny sausage and secure it at the top join of the scarf, cut to size and tuck in the ends.

14 Make the badges by taking small balls of red and blue paste, flattening and then attaching to the sleeve and front of the shirt with edible glue.

15 To make the head, follow the instructions on page 12 for a basic smiley face.

16 For the hair take the Golden Bear Brown Sugar Dough and divide into 1g and 2g portions. Out of the smaller ball of paste, cut out 2 triangles to go in front of the ears, mark with a Dresden tool and secure in place with edible glue. Shape the larger ball of paste into an oval, mark with a Dresden tool and attach to the head, leaving the top of the head clear for the cap. Shape the remaining paste into a sausage, flatten and mark with a Dresden tool. Glue to the front of the head so that it rests slightly over the triangles at the ears.

17 Divide the remaining dark green Sugar Dough into 2 portions of 4g and 2g. Shape the larger portion into a ball, push your thumb underneath and pinch the paste down to form a dome shape. Glue this to the top of the head. Roll the remaining paste into a sausage and flatten one side with your fingers to form a peak. Cut a straight edge along the thicker side and secure to the front of the cap with edible glue. Bring the sides of the peak down a little.

cub scout cupcake

To make the scarf you will need 5g (just under ¼oz) of White Sugar Dough, a tiny amount of Blue and 4g (just under ¼oz) of Red. Make the scarf as per the figure but cut 3 strips from the paste at an angle instead of 2. Curl one around into a loop and secure the triangle underneath with edible glue. Bend the scarf into shape and cross the ends over.

brownie

edibles

SK Sugar Dough: 28g (1oz) Brown, 10g (¼oz)
Golden Bear Brown, 20g (¾oz) Soft Beige, 3g
(small ball) White, 12g (just under ½oz) Yellow

SK Food Colour Pen: Brown

equipment

11.5cm (4½") long wooden barbeque skewer

Important note: Remember to remove the
wooden skewer before the model is eaten.

1 Divide the Brown Sugar Dough as follows:
8g for the shoes; 16g for the skirt; 3g for the
sleeves; and a pinch for the neck opening.

2 Divide the Soft Beige Sugar Dough as follows:
4g for the legs; 5g for the arms; 10g for the
head; and a small pinch for the neck.

3 Divide the paste for the shoes in half and
shape into 2 ovals. Push the end of a bone
tool into the top of each shoe towards the back for
the socks to fit into.

4 Divide the small ball of White Sugar Dough
into 2 uneven pieces to create one sock
smaller than the other. Shape each piece into
a cone, push the end of a paintbrush down the
centre of both and mark creases around the sides
with a Dresden tool. Use a little edible glue to
secure the socks inside the indents of the shoes.

5 Divide the paste for the legs into 2 uneven
pieces and shape into sausages with a
point at both ends. Brush a little edible glue on
the socks and then secure the legs into position

by pushing a leg into each sock. Ease a wooden skewer through one leg and into the shoe. Leave to dry.

6 Shape the skirt into a cone shape and mark the pleats of the skirt using a Dresden tool. Push a spare skewer through the base of the skirt and then remove. Use the end of a paintbrush to make this hole slightly larger and to make a hole for the other leg to fit into. Brush a little edible glue over the legs and on the top of the skirt and secure the skirt by placing it over the skewer. Leave this to dry for as long as possible.

7 Roll the Yellow Sugar Dough into a cone, then push your thumb into the underside of the cone and pinch down the paste between your finger and thumb. Push a spare skewer through the middle from the top and remove. Brush edible glue over the top of the skirt and ease the top over the skewer. Mark a couple of creases on either side of the top using a Dresden tool.

8 Divide the paste for the sleeves in half and roll each piece into a cone. Push the end of a paintbrush into the base of the cone so the arms can be attached later, then secure the sleeves to the body with a little edible glue and mark with a Dresden tool.

9 For the collar, shape a small pinch of the Brown Sugar Dough into a ball and pinch between your finger and thumb to make a disc. Brush a little edible glue over the top and secure to the body over the skewer.

10 Using a slightly smaller pinch of the Soft Beige Sugar Dough than was used for the collar, follow the above step and secure in place for the neck.

11 Roll each arm into a sausage, gently flatten each end between your finger and thumb and make an incision on one side of each hand with a small, sharp knife. Ease out the thumb and smooth over the cut edges. Cut the sausage in half and shape each cut end into a point to fit inside the sleeves. Mark the elbow of each arm with a Dresden tool and bend slightly. Secure into place with edible glue and bring the hands to the front of the body, one on top of the other.

12 To make the Brownie's head, follow the instructions on page 12 for a basic smiley face.

13 For the hair, divide the Golden Bear Brown Sugar Dough as follows: 4g for the back of the head; 2 x 2g for the sides of the head; and 2g for the fringe. Shape, mark with a Dresden tool and use edible glue to attach the hair to the head, smoothing over any joins with the Dresden tool.

14 Use a Brown Food Colour Pen to draw the 'Brownies' logo onto the front of the t-shirt.

brownie cupcake

Roll out 6g (just under ¼oz) of Yellow Sugar Dough and cut a 4cm (1½") circle. Roll cut 2g (pinch) of White Sugar Dough and cut a small star. Knead the trimmings together, take off a small ball and shape into a long teardrop for the base of the logo. Shape the remaining paste into a long, even sausage, round off the ends and curl it around to form the top of the logo, following the template as a guide. Secure the white pieces of paste to the yellow disc.

Where there's a celebration there's a cake! Finish yours off with some fun characters to suit the occasion, from birthdays and christenings to weddings and anniversaries.

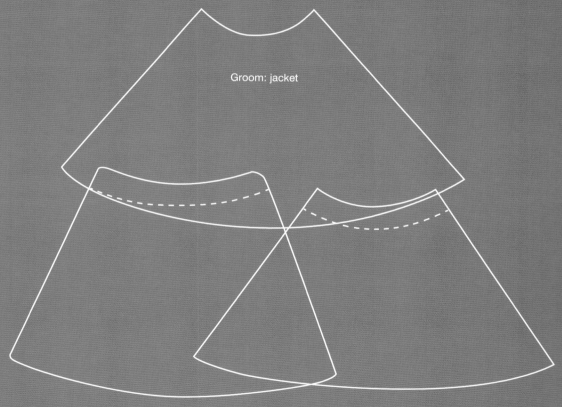

Groom: jacket

Elderly gent: jacket

Elderly lady: jacket

CELEBRATIONS

santa claus

edibles

SK Sugar Dough: 3g (just under ¼oz) Black, 35g (1¼oz) Golden Bear Brown, 125g (4½oz) Red, 35g (1¼oz) Soft Beige, 40g (1½oz) White

SK Food Colour Pen: Black

equipment

9cm (3½") wooden barbeque skewer

Important note: Remember to remove the wooden skewer before the model is eaten.

1 Divide the Red Sugar Dough as follows: 50g for the trousers; 40g for the jacket; 18g for the sleeves; and 15g for Santa's hat.

2 Divide the White Sugar Dough as follows: 5g for the beard; 4g for the moustache; 10g for the hair: 5g for the cuffs; 8g for the jacket; and 5g for the hat trim.

3 Roll the trousers into a wide sausage, making the middle slightly thicker than the ends. Bend the legs round towards the front slightly then mark creases over the trouser legs with a Dresden tool. Push the barbeque skewer down the centre to support the jacket and head.

4 For Santa's boots, use 30g of the Golden Bear Brown Sugar Dough and follow the instructions on page 16. Once made, secure one to the end of each trouser leg with edible glue. For the soles of the boots use 1g of Black Sugar Dough per boot, roll into an oval shape, flatten and secure to the underside of each boot. Mark the heel with the blunt edge of a small, sharp knife.

5 Make the jacket from Red Sugar Dough following the steps on page 20. Roll the White Sugar Dough for the jacket trim into a long sausage, mark with a Dresden tool and attach from the neck, down the front of the jacket and all around the base using edible glue. Cut to size at the front.

6 Make the belt with the remaining Golden Bear Brown Sugar Dough: roll out a strip and cut 2 straight edges 0.5cm apart. Cut off a 0.5cm square and reserve for the centre of the buckle. Attach the belt around the middle of the jacket, starting at the front, and cut to size. Use a little edible glue to attach the buckle into the centre. Roll out 1g of Black Sugar Dough, cut a slightly larger square from the Black Sugar Dough to create a border for the buckle then attach this to the front of the belt with edible glue.

7 To make the sleeves, follow the instructions for long sleeves on page 21. Secure to the top of the jacket with a little edible glue and bring them towards the front of the body. Roll the paste for the cuffs into a sausage shape and mark with a Dresden tool as before, then cut in half and attach around the end of each sleeve. Cut to size if necessary.

8 Use 2g of the Soft Beige Sugar Dough to make the hands, following the steps on page 21. Attach the hands to the body with a little edible glue so that they are resting on the buckle.

9 For the head roll 30g of Soft Beige Sugar Dough into a ball and push the end of a spare barbeque skewer into the base. Brush a little edible glue around the neck area, remove the skewer from the head and ease it over the skewer in the figure.

10 Shape the beard into a triangle, flatten slightly and mark with a Dresden tool. Attach halfway down the head with a little edible glue.

11 Divide the White Sugar Dough for the moustache into 2 and shape each piece into a teardrop. Mark with a Dresden tool and secure to the top of the beard with edible glue.

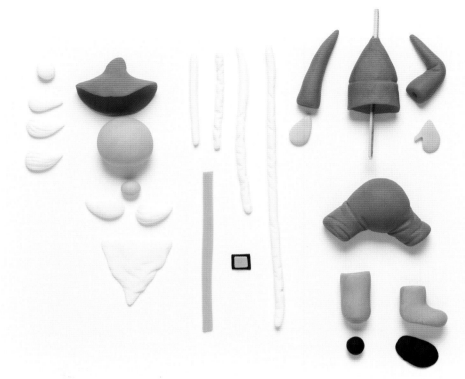

12 Next, draw the eyes and eyebrows on the face using the Black Food Colour Pen. For the nose, roll 1g of Soft Beige Sugar Dough into a ball and secure it to the front of the head in the centre of the moustache with a little edible glue.

13 Roll Santa's hat into a cone, push your thumb into the base and pinch out the paste to form the opening of the hat. Brush edible glue around the back of the head and attach the hat, leaving some space at the front for the hair to fit into. Mark the back of the hat with a Dresden tool and bend it upwards a little. Roll the White Sugar Dough for the hat trim into a long sausage and mark with a Dresden tool. Brush edible glue around the rim of the hat, secure the trim in place and cut to size at the neck edge.

14 Divide the paste for the hair into 7 pieces and shape into teardrops. Mark each piece with a Dresden tool and attach to the underside of the hat at the front with edible glue. Bend the hair pieces back over the trim.

christmas cupcakes

Christmas tree

Shape 12g (just over ¼oz) of Green Sugar Dough into a cone and push the end of a paintbrush into the underside of the paste. Take a small pair of sharp scissors and cut incisions from top to bottom, turning the cone after each cut. Ease the paste off the paintbrush carefully. Roll out 1g (small pinch) of Yellow Sugar Dough, cut a small star with a cutter and attach to the top of the tree with edible glue.

Santa's hat

You will need 15g (½oz) of Red Sugar Dough for the main part of the hat and 5g (just under ¼oz) of White Sugar Dough for the trim. Make the hat as for the figure, then add the trim and a ball at the top.

party fairy

edibles

SK Sugar Dough: 10g (¼oz) Brown, 18g (just under ¾oz) Orange, 33g (1¼oz) Soft Beige, 15g (½oz) White, 2g (pinch) Yellow

equipment

7.5cm (3") long wooden barbeque skewer

5.5cm (2¼") x 26-gauge floral wire: white

FMM: Small star cutter (FMM)

Butterfly wing cutter (TT)

Veining tool (optional)

Important note: Remember to remove the wooden skewer and wire before the model is eaten.

1 Divide the Soft Beige Sugar Dough as follows: 12g for the legs; 1g for the neck; 10g for the arms; and 10g for the head.

2 Divide the Orange Sugar Dough as follows: 2g for the shoes; 2g for the skirt; and 14g for the body.

3 Roll the paste for the legs into a sausage which is slightly wider in the middle, then bend it in half to bring the legs round to the front.

4 Divide the shoes into 2 equal pieces and pinch out a small piece from each for the strap. Roll the 2 larger pieces into ovals and push the end of a bone tool into the middle of each shoe towards the back. Secure the legs inside the shoes with edible glue. Roll out each small pinch of paste into a thin sausage, brush a little edible glue on either side of the shoe and attach the strap. Cut to size if necessary and push the end of a Dresden tool into the outside edge of the strap for the button fastening.

5 For the skirt, mix all of the White Sugar Dough with the reserved orange paste to make a pale orange colour. Roll out into a strip, then cut 2 straight edges 2.5cm apart. Use either a veining tool or the end of a paintbrush to frill around the edge of the strip. Gather the paste on one side, brush edible glue over the top of the legs and secure the gathered strip to form the skirt. Cut to size and fold under the ends at the back to hide any joins. Push the skewer into the centre of the skirt to help to hold the body and head in position.

6 To make the wings, knead together any remaining pale orange paste, roll out and cut out 2 wings with a cutter. Set aside to dry a little.

7 For the wand, roll out the Yellow Sugar Dough and cut a small star using a cutter. Dip the end of the white wire into the edible glue and push into the star.

8 Follow the steps on page 19 to make a leotard top from Orange Sugar Dough.

9 Divide the paste for the neck into 2 and roll both pieces into balls. Push the end of a spare skewer into the centre of each and remove. Brush a little edible glue around the neck area and ease one ball into place over the top over the skewer. Repeat with the second ball.

10 Follow the instructions on page 21 to make the arms and hands. Secure the hands at the front of the body with edible glue. Attach the wand behind the hands and the wings at the back of the body with edible glue.

11 Make the head in the style of a basic smiley face, see page 12.

12 Brush edible glue over the head where the hair will be placed and make curly hair following the instructions on page 15.

Remember to safely remove the wire and any paste that it has come into contact with it before the figure is eaten.

fairy present cupcake

You will need 18g (just under ¾oz) of Orange Sugar Dough and a mix of 3g (large pinch) each of Orange and White Sugar Dough for a paler orange. Shape the Orange Sugar Dough into a cube and set aside.

Roll out the paler orange paste and cut a strip to fit over the present both ways. Cut to size and secure to the cube using edible glue. Knead together the trimmings, roll out again and cut 2 short strips for the ribbon ends. Secure to the top of the present with edible glue. Cut another strip 4cm (1½") long and bring the ends around to the centre to form a bow. Make a small ball for the centre of the bow and mark with a Dresden tool. Secure the bow on top of the present.

bride

edibles

SK Sugar Dough: 5g (just under ¼oz) Green, 5g (just under ¼oz) Red; 26g (just under 1oz) Soft Beige, 94g (3oz) White, 12g (just under ½oz) Yellow

SK Food Colour Pens: Red, Black

equipment

12.5cm (5") wooden barbeque skewer

Important note: Remember to remove the wooden skewer before the model is eaten.

1 Divide the White Sugar Dough as follows: 2g for the shoes; 50g for the skirt; 25g for the train; 15g for the bodice; 2g for the bow; and a pinch for the eyes.

2 Divide the Soft Beige Sugar Dough as follows: 4g for the body; 10g for the arms; and 12g for the head.

3 To make the shoes, cut the paste in half and roll into triangles. Flatten one edge of the triangle and round off the pointed end.

4 To make the skirt, follow the instructions for the long skirt on page 18, secure the shoes at the front of the skirt and leave to dry for as long as possible, preferably overnight.

5 Roll out the paste for the train and cut out a paddle shape with a width of 3.5cm at the top. Attach this to the waist of the skirt with a little edible glue. Once secured, gather the bottom of the train by lifting the edges up and down and then create pleats by running a Dresden tool from top to bottom.

6 Follow the steps on page 20 to make the bodice for the bride. For the bow, roll out the Sugar Dough very thinly and cut out a 4cm long strip. Bring the ends into the centre to form the bow shape. Secure a long roll of the White Sugar Dough vertically in the middle of the bodice at the back with edible glue and attach the bow on top.

7 Roll the top of the body into a half-moon shape to fit inside the bride's bodice. Push a spare barbeque skewer through the middle, remove and secure into the bodice with edible glue.

8 Follow the steps on page 21 to make the arms. Secure the hands to the front of the skirt ready to hold the bouquet using a little edible glue.

9 Make the head according to the instructions for the smiley face on page 12 and draw on the lips using the Red Food Colour Pen. For the eyes, pinch out 2 small balls from the White Sugar Dough reserved earlier, flatten and attach above the nose. Push the end of a Black Food Colour Pen into each of the eyes for the pupils and then use the pen to draw on eyelashes.

10 To make the hair, roll 7g of Yellow Sugar Dough for the back of the head into a ball. Pinch the paste out all around the edges, leaving a ridge down the centre (this will form the French pleat). Mark the paste on either side of this with a Dresden tool for the hair, then mark over the ridge and push the end of a paintbrush into the top of the pleat. Secure to the back of the head and smooth the hair into the head around the edges for a neat finish.

11 Using the remaining Yellow Sugar Dough, make 2 triangles of paste, mark as before and attach to the head in front of the ears. Blend

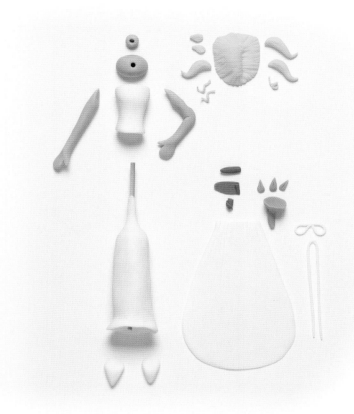

the paste into the back hair with a Dresden tool. Make tiny curls around the base of the hair at the neck and one either side of the head at the ears. Attach each one using the end of a Dresden tool and edible glue. For the fringe, make teardrop shapes, mark with a Dresden tool and curl up the ends. Secure to the top of the head.

12 To make the posy, take 2g of Green Sugar Dough and shape into a 'T'. Flatten the top and secure inside the bride's hands with edible glue.

13 For the leaves, make small teardrop shapes from 3g of Green Sugar Dough, mark down the centre of each one with the blunt edge of a small knife and pinch the tip to a point. Secure to the outer edge of the posy with edible glue. Make 3 extra leaves for the bride's hair and secure on top.

14 Pinch the Red Sugar Dough into small balls and then roll into small sausages. Roll out the paste, lift off with a palette knife then roll the paste into a spiral to make a rose. Cut to size at the base and secure inside the posy and leaves with edible glue. Attach 3 roses to the top of the bride's head between the leaves.

bride cupcake

Model 10g (¼oz) of White Sugar Dough into a triangle, then flatten and extend 2 corners and bend them around into a tiara shape. Use a Dresden tool to make small indents across the top of the tiara, then mark the front with perforations. Dust the tiara with SK Magic Sparkles Metallic Lustre Dust.

groom

edibles

SK Sugar Dough: 80g (2¾oz) Black, 8g (¼oz) Brown, 1g (small pinch) Green, 3g (just under ¼oz) Red, 15g (½oz) Soft Beige, 30g (1oz) White

equipment

14cm (5½") wooden barbeque skewer

Template for jacket (see page 74)

Important note: Remember to remove the wooden skewer before the model is eaten.

1 Divide the Black Sugar Dough as follows: 12g for the shoes; 30g for the trousers; 20g for the jacket; 2g for the collar; 15g for the sleeves; and 1g for the waistcoat.

2 Divide the White Sugar Dough as follows: 20g for the shirt; 8g for the waistcoat; and 2g for the collar.

3 Divide the Soft Beige Sugar Dough as follows: 1g for the neck; 2g for the hands; and 12g for the head.

4 Divide the paste for the shoes into 2 and shape into ovals.

5 Follow the steps on page 18 to make the trousers in Black Sugar Dough. Brush edible glue over the top of both shoes and secure the skewer in the leg into one of the shoes. Allow to dry, preferably overnight.

6 Shape the White Sugar Dough for the shirt into a cone. Push your thumb into the wide end of the paste and pinch the paste down all around the base. Push a spare barbeque skewer down through

the centre of the shirt, remove and secure the shirt over the skewer in the legs with edible glue.

7 For the cravat, shape 2g of the Red Sugar Dough into a triangle and mark with a Dresden tool. Secure to the front of the shirt with edible glue.

8 Roll the Soft Beige Sugar Dough for the neck into a ball and push it over the skewer, attaching it to the top of the shirt and cravat with edible glue.

9 For the waistcoat, mix the White and Black Sugar Dough together to make a grey colour. Roll out and cut a 'V' for a neck opening, mark down the centre with the blunt edge of a small, sharp knife and then cut a 'W' at the base of the waistcoat. Secure to the front of the shirt up against the base of the cravat with edible glue.

10 Roll out the White Sugar Dough for the collar and cut a strip 0.5cm wide to fit around the neck. Cut to size then cut the ends

at an angle. Secure with edible glue and turn the corners downwards. Leave this to dry for as long as possible, preferably overnight.

11 Roll out the Black Sugar Dough for the jacket and cut out the shape using the template. Secure to the back of the figure and fold back the lapels.

12 To finish the collar, roll out the Black Sugar Dough and cut a rectangle to fit the back of the neck between the lapels. Secure into place with edible glue.

13 Follow the steps on page 21 to make the jacket sleeves, bend one arm and leave the other straight.

14 For the rose and leaves, roll 2 small balls of Green Sugar Dough and a small ball of Red Sugar Dough. Shape the 2 green pieces into teardrops, pinch between your finger and thumb and mark down the centre of both with the blunt side of a small knife. Pinch the tips of the leaves and secure to one of the lapels with edible glue. Roll the red paste into a small sausage, roll out flat and lift off with a palette knife. Roll up the paste from one end to the other, cut down to size and secure between the leaves with edible glue.

15 Divide the Sugar Dough for the hands in 2 and follow the steps on page 21 to make the hands. Brush edible glue inside each of the sleeve ends and secure the hands in place, resting one on the waistcoat.

16 Using 12g of Soft Beige Sugar Dough, make a head with a cheerful face (see page 13).

17 For the groom's hair divide the Brown Sugar Dough as follows: 3g for the back of the head; 2 small triangles to go in front of the ears; and divide the remaining paste for the fringe pieces. Shape the hair for the back of the head into a ball, flatten into a disc and mark with a Dresden tool. Brush over the head with edible glue and secure the marked disc in place. Mark the 2 triangles, secure in front of the ears and smooth the paste into the hair at the back to hide the joins. Pinch out small pieces of Brown Sugar Dough, shape into teardrops, mark with a Dresden tool and secure to the top of the head. Lift the ends of the hair upwards a little and continue until the top of the head is covered.

groom cupcake

Use 15g (½oz) of Black Sugar Dough for the main part of the top hat and 7g (just under ¼oz) for the brim of the hat. Shape the top hat into a fat sausage with 2 flat ends. Roll the paste for the brim of the hat into a ball, flatten and attach to the centre of the top hat with edible glue. Curl the brim of the hat up a little on either side.

elderly gent

edibles

SK Sugar Dough: 2g (pinch) Black, 72g (2½oz)
Brown, 8g (¼oz) White, 12g (just under ½oz) Soft
Beige

SK Mexican Modelling Paste (MMP): 21g (¾oz)
Cream Celebration

equipment

12.5cm (5") wooden barbeque skewer

Template for jacket (see page 74)

Important note: Remember to remove the
wooden skewer before the model is eaten.

1 Divide the Brown Sugar Dough as follows:
12g for the shoes; 30g for the trousers; 12g
for the jacket; 10g for the sleeves; 7g for the hat;
and 1g for the bowtie.

2 Divide the Soft Beige Sugar Dough as
follows: 10g for the head; 1g for the neck
and 1g for the hands.

3 To make the shoes, divide the paste equally
and shape into 2 ovals.

4 For the legs, follow the instructions on page
18 for making trousers and leave to dry.

5 To make the shirt, follow the steps on page
20. Using a small knife, make a small
opening at the front of the shirt for a pocket.

6 Roll the Soft Beige Sugar Dough for the
neck into a small ball and flatten into a disc
between your finger and thumb. Brush a little
edible glue over the top of the shirt and secure
the neck to the body over the barbeque skewer.

7 Take a small amount of Cream MMP for the shirt collar and roll out. Cut a strip measuring 0.5cm wide and cut each end at an angle. Secure around the neck with edible glue, leaving the collar ends pointing upwards until the bowtie has been attached.

8 For the bowtie, divide the paste into 3: roll a small ball for the centre of the tie and 2 equal triangles for the bow. Attach these triangles at the neck and mark with a Dresden tool towards the centre. Next, roll the small ball into a sausage, flatten and secure over the centre of the bow, tucking the ends in with a Dresden tool. Bring the ends of the collar down a little over the tie.

9 Roll out the paste for the jacket and cut out the shape following the template. Secure this around the body with edible glue, then curl the collar back a little.

10 Roll the Brown Sugar Dough for the sleeves into a sausage and taper the ends to a rounded point. Cut the length in half equally, mark the elbows with a Dresden tool and bend one arm slightly. Push the end of a paintbrush into the cut end for the hands to be secured into. Brush edible glue on either side of the jacket, attach the sleeves to the jacket and mark the tops with a Dresden tool.

11 Follow the steps on page 21 to make the hands.

12 To make the man's head, follow the instructions on page 14. When you are making the hair, mix the White Sugar Dough with a small pinch of Black Sugar Dough to make a grey colour. Follow the steps 2 and 3 for the man's head but leave the top of the head clear for a hat to be placed onto (if required).

elderly gent 89

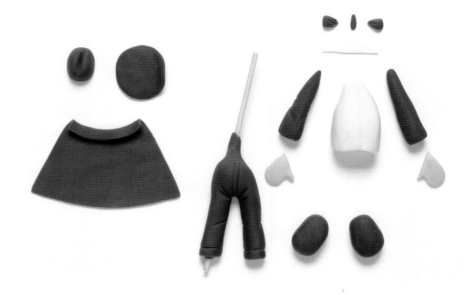

13 Divide the Brown Sugar Dough reserved for the hat into 2 portions of 3g and 4g. Take the smaller portion for the brim of the hat, roll into a ball, flatten and secure to the top of the head with a little edible glue. Once in place, lift the sides and the front upwards a little. Use the remaining paste for the top of the hat, shape into a ball then rub on a flat surface to flatten the base. Pinch the top a little and run a Dresden tool from the middle towards the back. Secure to the head centrally on the brim with edible glue.

anniversary cupcakes

Silver wedding anniversary

Roll out 5g (just under ¼oz) of White Sugar Dough and cut the numbers 2 and 5 using a number cutter set. Leave to dry then dust all over with SK Silver Metallic Lustre Dust.

Golden wedding anniversary

Follow the same method as for the silver anniversary but use the numbers 5 and 0 and dust with SK Antique Gold Metallic Lustre Dust.

elderly lady

edibles

SK Sugar Dough: 2g (pinch) Black, 1g (small pinch) Blue, 12g (just under ½oz) Soft Beige, 37g (1¼oz) Violet, 13g (½oz) White

SK Mexican Modelling Paste (MMP): 20g (¾oz) Cream Celebration, 8g (¼oz) Teddy Bear Brown

equipment

11.5cm (4½") long wooden barbeque skewer

Jacket template (see page 74)

Important note: Remember to remove the wooden skewer before the model is eaten.

1 Divide the Violet Sugar Dough as follows: 8g for the skirt; 4g for the handbag; 20g for the jacket; and 5g for the hat.

2 Divide the Cream Celebration MMP as follows: 4g for the tights; 15g for the blouse; and 1g for the collar.

3 Divide the Soft Beige Sugar Dough as follows: 2g for the hands and 10g for the head.

4 Using the Teddy Bear Brown MMP, follow the steps on page 17 to make a pair of pointed shoes.

5 Roll the paste for the tights into a sausage and cut into 2 equal halves. Shape each end into a point and push the skewer through the centre of one of the sausages and into a shoe, securing the shoe in place with edible glue. Attach the other sausage into the shoe with a little edible glue.

6 Mix 8g of White Sugar Dough with the Violet to make a slightly paler purple colour, then follow the instructions on page 18 to make the lady's skirt. Use edible glue to attach the skewered leg

to the underneath of the skirt and pinch the paste around the top of the skirt to secure to the skewer. Push the end of a paintbrush into the underside of the skirt and secure the second leg into place using edible glue. Leave to dry.

7 Reserve a small ball of the paste for the handbag to make the handles. Shape the handbag into a square and use a sharp knife to make markings on the front of the bag. To make the handles, roll the Sugar Dough into a sausage, flatten it then cut the long edges straight. Attach to either side of the bag with edible glue, mark with the end of a Dresden tool three times to secure them in place and set aside to dry.

8 Roll the blouse into a cone shape, push your thumb into the base and pinch the paste around the edge. Push a spare barbeque skewer through the middle, remove and then attach the blouse to the skirt using a little edible glue.

Narrow the waist between your fingers and thumb to form a bust and mark the buttons with the end of a spare skewer. Mark 2 dart lines at the front starting from under the bust with a Dresden tool.

9 Roll out half of the Violet Sugar Dough for the jacket and cut to size using the template. Roll back the neck a little to form a collar and secure to the body using edible glue.

10 To make the sleeves, roll the remaining Violet Sugar Dough into a sausage shape and follow the instructions on page 21 for long sleeves. Bend both arms slightly, mark the tops of the shoulders with a Dresden tool and ease the jacket collar down a little over the top of the shoulders.

11 Roll the paste for the blouse collar into a ball, pinch into a disc and make an incision in the centre with a knife. Smooth over the cut edge and push over the skewer, securing to the top of the blouse with edible glue.

12 For the hands, follow the instructions on page 21. Secure the handbag into one of the hands using edible glue, holding in place until secured.

13 Follow the instructions on page 14 to make a woman's head but add in more wrinkles to the face using a Dresden tool and add light blue eyes to the face instead of brown.

14 Make the hair by mixing 5g of White Sugar Dough with a small pinch of Black Sugar Dough to make a grey colour. Take 2 small balls of this for the hair in front the ears and divide the remaining into 2 for the back of the hair and the fringe. Shape the 2 smaller balls into triangles, mark roughly with a Dresden tool and attach to the head in front of the ears. Roll the 2 remaining pieces into sausages, mark as before and attach to the front and back of the head, leaving the top of the head clear to affix a hat.

15 Roll the Violet Sugar Dough for the hat into a ball and flatten into a disc 1.5cm thick. Push your thumb into the underside and pinch out the paste to fit over the top of the head. Secure in place with edible glue.

baby

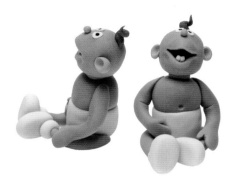

edibles

SK Sugar Dough: 2g (pinch) Blue, 1g (small
pinch) Black, 1g (small pinch) Brown, 32g (just
over 1oz) White

SK MMP: 12g (just under ½oz) Teddy Bear Brown

equipment

6.5cm (2½") long wooden barbeque skewer

Important note: Remember to remove the
wooden skewer before the model is eaten.

1 Divide the White Sugar Dough as follows: 19g
for the pants and bootees; 12g to mix the skin
tone; and 1g for the eyes and teeth.

2 To make the olive skin tone, mix 12g of White
Sugar Dough with the same amount of Teddy
Bear Brown MMP. Divide this as follows: 3g for the
legs; 9g for the body, 4g for the arms and 8g for the
head.

3 To make the pants, mix 19g of White Sugar
Dough with a little Blue Sugar Dough to make
a pale blue colour. Divide this into 2 equal parts and
hold one half back to make the bootees later. Roll
the paste for the pants into a ball, push into the top
of the ball with your thumb and pinch up the paste
to form a smooth cup which will hold the body.

4 For the bootees, divide the paste in half again,
pinch out a small amount from each half and
roll into 2 balls for the ankles. Shape the remainder
into 2 ovals and brush a little edible glue over the
back of these. Push the end of a paintbrush into
the centre of the small balls and attach to the glued
area on the oval paste.

5 Roll the legs into a sausage, making both ends slightly pointed. Cut this through the centre at an angle using a sharp knife. Secure the angled end of the legs to each side of the pants with a little edible glue. Next, brush a little of the glue inside each bootee and push the pointed end of the legs inside to secure. Bend one leg around to the front of the body and leave one straight.

6 Roll the body into a ball and secure inside the top of the pants with edible glue. Use the end of a paintbrush to make a bellybutton at the front. Roll a small pinch of the flesh coloured Sugar Dough to make the baby's neck, brush a little edible glue onto the top of the body and push a wooden skewer into the neck. Secure the neck to the body by twisting the skewer down through the body and the pants; this will support the baby's head.

7 Follow the steps on page 21 to make the baby's arms. Secure the arms to the body using edible glue, resting one on the bent leg and the other on top of the bootee.

8 Make the head by following the instructions for the toddler on page 14. Secure the head to the body over the neck and skewer with a little edible glue.

9 Roll a pinch of the Brown Sugar Dough into a teardrop shape and cut the larger end at an angle with a sharp knife. Secure to the top of the head with a little edible glue and curl to make the hair.

To make a baby girl, simply make the pants and bootees pale pink instead of blue and do the same on the cupcake decoration. Remember that you can change the skin tone, hair colour and facial expression to personalise your sugar baby.

baby cupcakes

Bootees

Make the bootees as for the figure using 14g (½oz) of White Sugar Dough mixed with a small amount of Blue Sugar Dough (or Red for a girl).

Footprints

Mix 4g (just under ¼oz) of White Sugar Dough with a tiny amount of Blue paste (or Red to make a soft pink colour). Divide the paste in half, then from each piece pinch out 5 toes going from the big toe and getting smaller towards the little toe. Roll each one into a ball and flatten. Shape the 2 remaining pieces of paste into ovals, flatten and make a small indent on one side of the foot with your finger. Position the toes above the foot.

suppliers

Squires Kitchen, UK

3 Waverley Lane
Farnham
Surrey
GU9 8BB
0845 61 71 810
+44 1252 260 260
www.squires-shop.com

Squires Kitchen International School

The Grange
Hones Yard
Farnham
Surrey
GU9 8BB
0845 61 71 812
+44 1252 260 262
www.squires-school.co.uk

Squires Kitchen, France

+33 (0) 1 82 88 01 66
clientele@squires-shop.fr
www.squires-shop.fr

Squires Kitchen, Spain

+34 93 180 7382
cliente@squires-shop.es
www.squires-shop.es

SK stockists

Jane Asher Party Cakes
London
020 7584 6177

Blue Ribbons
Surrey
020 8941 1591

Catering Complements
Kent
01892 513745

Lawsons Ltd.
Devon
01752 892543

The Sugarcraft Emporium
Worcestershire
01527 576703

Surbiton Art & Sugarcraft
Surrey
020 8391 4664

SK distributors

Guy Paul & Co. Ltd.
Buckinghamshire
www.guypaul.co.uk

Culpitt Ltd.
Northumberland
NE63 8UQ
www.culpitt.com

manufacturers

Smeg UK Ltd.
www.smeguk.com
www.smeg50style.com
Italian appliance manufacturer
Smeg produces distinctive
domestic appliances combining
design, performance and quality.

Ribbon Packaging

Papillon
RIBBON

Rick Kong

rickkong@papillonuk.com

Papillon Ribbon & Bow (U.K.) Ltd
22 Dalston Gardens
Stanmore
Middlesex. HA7-1BU
United Kingdom

Tel 0208-206-1898
Fax 0208-206-1218

www.papillonribbon.com